THINK RED

Think Red

Imagine Your Community
Living and Loving Like Jesus

LARRY STOESS

 CASCADE *Books* • Eugene, Oregon

THINK RED
Imagine Your Comminity Living and Loving Like Jesus

Cascade Books
An Imprint of Wipf and Stock Publishers
199 W. 8th Ave., Suite 3
Eugene, OR 97401

www.wipfandstock.com

PAPERBACK ISBN: 978-1-7252-7167-8
HARDCOVER ISBN: 978-1-7252-7166-1
EBOOK ISBN: 978-1-7252-7168-5

Cataloguing-in-Publication data:

Names: Stoess, Larry, author.
Title: Think red : imagine your community living and loving like Jesus / Larry Stoess.
Description: Eugene, OR: Cascade Books, 2021 | Includes bibliographical references.
Identifiers: ISBN 978-1-7252-7167-8 (paperback) | ISBN 978-1-7252-7166-1 (hardcover) | ISBN 978-1-7252-7168-5 (ebook)
Subjects: LCSH: Church development, New. | Mission of the church. |
Classification: BV652.24 .S80 2021 (print) | BV652 (ebook)

This book is dedicated to my neighbors in Portland,
Who made the story worth telling
&
My wife Kathie,
Who made living the story a mysterious joy.

*I used to believe faith was being certain about the mysteries of God,
but now I marvel at mystery and try to remain faithful
in a life filled with uncertainty.*

CONTENTS

Introduction

IN 1975, A CHRISTIAN songwriter named John Fischer wrote a catchy little tune called "Evangelical Veil Productions." The first time I heard the song was on a hillside in Kentucky at an outdoor music festival. I was a new Christian, extremely excited about my decision to follow Jesus, and ready to share my newfound faith with the rest of the world.

The song was a satire about evangelical church people like me, with a playful jab at hypocrisy in the church. I loved the song and would laugh inside every time I sang along with my vinyl record player.

> Evangelical Veil Productions,
> Pick one up now at quite a reduction
> Got all types of shapes and sizes,
> Introductory bonus prizes.
> Special quality one-way see through,
> You can see them but they can't see you.
> Never have to show yourself again.

Forty years later I'm still following Jesus. I'm still madly in love with my wife, Kathie, who was by my side when I sat on the hill and listened to John Fischer sing folk songs about Jesus. And I still love to share my faith with anyone who wants to listen. But much has changed in the evangelical church over the past forty years and I'm not laughing anymore.

Somewhere along the way the word *evangelical* got hijacked and the evangelical Jesus People that captured my heart in the seventies began to confuse radical faith in Jesus with nationalism and traded a countercultural movement for consumer-driven religion. The list of social and theological woes that sidelined the evangelical church is a rather long list. In response, the dominant culture has placed the evangelical church on mute; the church is still proclaiming a message, but who's listening?

Here's the dilemma I'm faced with and the purpose of this book: I love my evangelical heritage and I'm convinced more than ever that the good news Jesus proclaimed to the poor is the most relevant message for the world today. I believe the goodness of God, revealed in the life, death, and resurrection of Jesus can restore life to broken individuals and redeem unjust social systems. But the social and theological blunders of the evangelical church have created a religious fog that prevents this good news from being heard and received by those who need it most.

How then, do we—those who want to follow the way of Jesus—proclaim his good news to the poor? How do we pursue the vision of Jesus— a vision where the blind see and the oppressed are set free? How do we live out the mission of Jesus—giving all we have to love God and love our neighbors? My desire to discover faithful and honest answers to questions such as these compelled me to write this book. But I fear half the people reading this introduction will hear the word *evangelical* and lay the book aside; the other half may read my critique of the evangelical church and begin looking around for a box of matches.

If you choose to read on, you may discover a fresh and exciting way to proclaim the gospel of Jesus by living out your faith in a beloved community—a community whose constitution is built around the values of Jesus; not just in word, but in deed.[1] There is a new movement of the Holy Spirit making its way across the landscape of the church. The prophetic leaders of the movement remind me of those reminiscent radical Christians who led the Jesus movement in the seventies. They are taking Jesus seriously and actually believe he meant for us to do the things he said. Because of the ambiguity, or should I say toxicity, around the word *evangelical*, the leaders of this movement prefer to be identified as Red Letter Christians. Their name draws on the fact that many Bibles print the words of Jesus in red. They want to make the words and the ways of Jesus central to the way

1. "Beloved Community" is a term popularized by Dr. Martin Luther King Jr., to describe his vision for a society based on justice, equal opportunity, and love. His vision, as explained by The King Center, "is a global vision in which all people can share in the wealth of the earth . . . [P]overty, hunger and homelessness will not be tolerated because international standards of human decency will not allow it. Racism and all forms of discrimination, bigotry and prejudice will be replaced by an all-inclusive spirit of sisterhood and brotherhood" (see https://thekingcenter.org/#the-beloved-community). In this book I will use the term *beloved community* to define a community whose constitution is built around the values of Jesus; some of the values discussed in this book are reminiscent of Dr. King's vision for society.

they live and organize their communities. They want a Christianity that looks like Jesus.[2]

The dream of seeing an increase of individuals and communities that passionately pursue what I call the Red Letter Mission of Jesus is the hope I have for writing this book. Over the past twenty years, Kathie and I have lived in the same community, with a beautiful and diverse mix of Jesus followers. Some of us landed in Portland (an inner-city neighborhood on the northwest corner of Louisville, Kentucky) because of our faith in Jesus. Others were born here and made a decision to remain even when many of their friends and neighbors made the choice to move up and out. Even though we never called ourselves Red Letter Christians, we have been carried along by the vision of developing a Christian community around the values of Jesus.

Building a beloved community around the values of Jesus is easier to dream about and reflect on than to actually live out. Following Jesus together, on a mission to love God and love our neighbors, really is a trial-and-error, learn-as-you-go, build-the-bridge-as-you-walk-on-it kind of experience. It takes time and effort, and a steady diet of soul-searching practices. Over the years I have been encouraged and challenged by reading stories from other Christian Community Developers. I hope this book, with anecdotes from our experience, will provide the same encouragement for you.

In the chapters that follow we will "Think Red" together and explore the Red Letter Values of Jesus, as well as his Red Letter Vision and Red Letter Mission. The first six chapters will highlight the values our community identified as organizing principles for our common life: the value of love and friendship, downward mobility, affirming the dignity of all people, radical generosity, and the value of small beginnings and new beginnings. Some of these values are obvious to the casual reader of the Gospels and discovered by listening to the things Jesus talked about and the stories he told. Others are not so obvious, and are brought to light by observing the way Jesus behaved with people and the choices he made. Each chapter will explore one of the six values, give a biblical foundation to support the value, and provide specific examples of how the value guided and influenced our missional community in Portland.

In chapter 7 we will explore the Red Letter Vision Jesus had for the future. He saw a preferred future different from the current reality of the

2. See Redletterchristians.org.

world he lived in. He called his preferred future the kingdom of God. He knew the kingdom was near and was pressing into his current reality, but it was not yet revealed in its full expression. There was more to come. Those who follow Jesus will embrace his vision as their own. They will pray like he taught us to pray, asking that the kingdom of God come on earth as it is in heaven. And they will seek creative ways to be an answer to their prayers.

With the values of Jesus and his vision set as a backdrop, chapter 8 will reflect on the Red Letter Mission of Jesus and subsequently the mission of a community based on his values. What did Jesus do? What was his plan? What was his strategy for bringing his vision to reality? What in the world did he have in mind when he dreamed up the church and commissioned the first disciples as his primary mission strategy? The answer to these questions will help you creatively imagine how to live on mission with Jesus in your context.

The new commandment Jesus gave, to love God and love one another, and the commission he gave, to make disciples, can empower a very fluid and flexible enterprise. For some reason Christendom has narrowed the mission of the church to something very static and flat. When we traditionally think about the mission of the church we think about doing church programs, for church people, on church property.[3] We think about church meetings and worship gatherings. *Think Red* will challenge that narrow and static idea and suggest that the church is free to explore and experiment with creative and whimsical expressions of community.

Each chapter will conclude with red-letter questions. The questions are intended to engage you in a discussion with the Spirit of Christ about your community more than a discussion about the content of the book. As you reflect on the questions at the end of each chapter I encourage you to prayerfully assume Jesus is speaking directly to you. He really does expect us to try to do the things he did and to live out the things he said. The good news is this: he is willing and available to give you the courage and the power to give it a whirl if you will simply value what he valued and take him seriously.

A Red Rose

Before we jump into the book let me give you a little background of our story. When Kathie and I first moved from our "safe" and quiet home on

3. McNeal, *Kingdom Come*, 5-6.

the east end of town to live on the more "restless" west side of our city, we said to one another, "We'll live here for five years and then move on." The five-year plan grew into a lifelong adventure. We've lived in the Portland neighborhood for twenty-two years now, and we cannot imagine a better place on the planet to live.

However, when people visit our neighborhood for the first time, they usually notice the obvious signs of disinvestment: vacant lots filled with trash, boarded-up houses, broken glass on the sidewalks, graffiti on street signs, abandoned sofas and busted TVs scattered along the alleys. To be honest, when I first started driving into the neighborhood, that's all I noticed. I would commute in from my suburban home every day to hang out with teenagers at 1831 Baird Street. Baird Street is an obscure alley that sits between Portland Avenue and Bank Street. In the middle of the block there was a less-than-modest shotgun house. "Less-than-modest" is a more than generous description. "Substandard" or "rundown" would better define the building.

The little dilapidated house would come to be called the Portland Promise Center, a big name for such a small enterprise. The house had two old library tables for tutoring children, a cabinet with some board games, a ping-pong table, and an old stereo fully equipped with an eight-track tape player. The office was tucked away in the furnace room. The kitchen was tiny and dark, with a ceiling covered in brown stains, betraying the multiple leaks in the roof. The bathroom floor settled over the years and landed at a twenty-six degree angle. It was so out of level you had to hold onto the sink if you didn't want to fall off the toilet. But the kids in the neighborhood loved the place.

And so did we. Every day, Kathie and I would greet volunteers from around the city to help kids with their homework. We would play a little ping-pong, eat some out-of-date butter cookies left in the pantry by the local food bank, read a Bible story to the children, and then head for home. With the city skyline in our rearview mirror we would return to our ranch house in the suburbs, fix a glass of iced tea, and watch the sun set over the neighbor's dairy farm. The disparity of the two environments was unsettling. It was unsettling because we were falling in love with the city and the kids who lived there. Our hearts were being drawn to the city.

I remember well the day I was driving in to meet with my newfound friends and noticed something I had overlooked all summer. There on the corner of Eighteenth and Baird Street was a rose bush. A huge red rose was hanging over the chain-link fence, unfolding right before my eyes. The lawn was well manicured. The paint on the house was a cheerful light blue with lace curtains hanging in the window. The home was lovely and peaceful. How did I miss seeing this beautiful home all summer? As I pondered the question, I came to the conclusion it was because of the pit bull that lived next door. The pit bull's house had a refrigerator sitting on the front porch and broken windowpanes with soiled blankets for curtains. Along the fencerow was a dirt path where the pit bull ran back and forth in the front yard taunting every passerby, daring them to set foot on his property. Yes, it's possible that the combination of the "Beware of Dog" sign hanging cockeyed on the gate and the man-eating beast on the other side of the fence caused me to rush past the beautiful shotgun house next door; but if I'm truthful with myself, I think the reason goes a little deeper.

Our eyes have a way of deceiving our heart—or maybe it's the other way around. Perhaps it is our heart that betrays our eyes. Jesus said what is in the heart is revealed in the words we speak.[4] I think the same is true about our eyes. What's in our heart has a way of filtering what we see and how we view other people, especially others who live in a culture different from our own.

More often than we realize or would like to admit, our implicit attitudes and our ethnocentric, psychosocial constructs—not to mention our hidden fears and personal insecurities—prevent us from seeing the other as God sees them or as they truly are. I wasn't looking for red roses and pretty houses. I was looking for the poor and pitiful. I was expecting to see people in need of my help. I, like many people of privilege, came to the city with answers and solutions for the social problems I was seeing. My implicit bias prevented me from seeing the beauty of the place called Portland and the giftedness of the people who called Portland home. From the day I stopped and smelled the rose at the corner of Eighteenth and Baird Street I have seen my neighborhood in a totally different light.

Life in Portland has been one learning experience after another. My perspective on the kingdom of God has been enlarged and enriched by my neighbors, especially by those who have been a part of our beloved community called Church of the Promise.

Our life in Portland has been a gift of grace from the heart of God. I have learned to honor and truly love diversity. I have grown in my desire to see reflections of God's handiwork in every person I meet and every place

4. Luke 6:45.

I go. Portland has taught me over and over that the sacred is tucked away in the secular, like a rose reaching through a chain-link fence longing to be noticed; or, like a treasure hidden in a field, waiting for someone to stumble over it and recognize its worth. Our life in Portland has been a lifelong treasure hunt, discovering one beautiful expression after another of God's delightful kingdom.

I invite you to come with me, and let's "think red" together as you read about the valuable treasures we discovered in Portland. Who knows? You might discover some overlooked treasures in your neighborhood.

1

Love and Friendship

"Love the Lord your God with all your heart and with all your soul and with all your strength and with all your mind; and, love your neighbor as yourself."

JESUS

"I no longer call you servants, because a servant does not know his master's business. Instead, I have called you friends, for everything that I learned from my Father I have made known to you."

JESUS

VALUES INFLUENCE OUR ACTIONS, maybe more than we realize. The values held by a community of faith, or any group of people for that matter, will determine the culture of the community. If the community wants to organize itself for a specific purpose, the effectiveness of the community will be impacted, for better or worse, by the culture of the community and the leader's ability to create alignment around common values. The authors of *Managing by Values* claim, "When people align around shared values and unite in a common purpose, ordinary people can accomplish extraordinary results."[1] I believe their claim to be true. However, creating alignment in any organization, especially a volunteer group of folks coming

1. Blanchard and O'Connor, *Managing by Values*, 144.

from diverse social, cultural, and economic backgrounds, is no easy task. It takes time and what Eugene Peterson calls "passionate patience."[2] Leaders in the community must have a burning passion around stated values that are actually practiced and lived out patiently and persistently over a long period of time. The stated values must be more than a list of virtues printed on a website. They must be practiced and rehearsed in real time. Trust and honor between members in the community must run deep because creating alignment around preferred values will require an ongoing conversation with honest processes for evaluation. Do we really value the things we say we value? Is there a gap between our stated values and our real values, those that are defined by our actions? What must we do to narrow the gap between the two and create alignment around the preferred values?

In my experience, if a community aligns its values with the values of Jesus, and if they embrace his vision and mission, the community will begin to look like Jesus. The creative potential of the community and its ability to bless the common good of a neighborhood or a city will increase exponentially. To test the thesis, the community and its leaders must first discern the core values of Jesus and then summon the courage to align their values with his. An honest assessment of the words and ways of Jesus will reveal how countercultural he was when compared to the ways of the world. Therefore, it will take courage, plus a will fortified with faith, and hope fueled with passion, in order to practice the values of Jesus in our twenty-first-century context.

Discerning the Core Values of Jesus

If you ever wonder what you really value, over and above what you say you value, take an inventory of your actions, specifically in two areas: How do you spend your money? And, how do you schedule your time? For instance, when the credit card bill arrives in my mailbox, you can make a safe bet a majority of the charges will be from the hardware store around the corner, revealing to Kathie that I bought another new tool or some building material for my latest project. The truth is, I value new tools and I like to build stuff. If you want to know how I spend my time, take a look at my calendar and you'll see on most days I schedule lunch meetings with friends. I like to eat; but who wants to eat alone? When my children were young and

2. Peterson, *Long Obedience*, 132.

someone asked in their presence what I did for a living, they would say, "He meets and eats."

Jesus didn't have a checkbook, but we know something about his economic values. He told a would-be-follower, "Foxes have dens and birds have nests, but the Son of Man has no place to lay his head."[3] Jesus isn't complaining about his financial position; he's simply stating a fact. The Son of Man made an intentional economic decision to be homeless so he could live in solidarity with the poor and better fulfill the work God sent him to accomplish. Neither did Jesus have a day-planner, but we know how he spent his time. Flip open the gospel story to any page, and you'll discover Jesus investing his time and energy in people or spending time alone with God. Above all else Jesus valued relationships. If you analyze the interpersonal encounters of Jesus, you discover that he gave his time and attention to three relationship networks.[4]

Jesus valued his friendship with God, whom he called Father. He valued his friendship with those who followed him, his disciples whom he regarded as family. And Jesus valued those forgotten and overlooked by society; namely, the poor. He had a special affinity with people who were marginalized and neglected. He referred to them as "the least of these" and identified with them to the point of saying, when you spend time with the poor, you are spending time with me. Jesus is so crazy in love with people he even values his enemies and challenges those who would follow him to do the same. The core value of Jesus, above all others, is love! A love for God and a love for people! But there is more: Love, Jesus-style, will create a seedbed for genuine and authentic friendship.

Chasing after the core values of love and friendship, and giving it everything we've got, is central when following the way of Jesus. Love God and love your neighbor! Following the way of Jesus really is that simple, but it's not so easy to pull off. Let's take a closer look at how Jesus cultivated friendship with God, friendship with the family of God, and friendship with the forgotten.

Friendship With God

The names and metaphors we use to describe our concept of God reveal much about our relationship with God. For instance, if I have a theological

3. Matt 8:20.

4. Breen, *Building a Discipling Culture*, 67.

chat with a friend, and they point to the sky and refer to God as "The Big Guy Upstairs," it's a pretty good indicator that my friend doesn't have a very intimate friendship with God. Nobody refers to their friend as The Big Guy That Lives Over There, unless they are trying to distinguish their big friend from the little one that lives in the other direction.

There are numerous metaphors in the Bible describing the multifaceted nature of God: counselor, comforter, judge, rock, refuge, a mother hen, and an ever-present help in time of trouble, to name a few. For Jesus, the primary metaphor he used to describe his relationship with God was Abba, the Aramaic term for Father. In the New Testament, Jesus refers to God as the Heavenly Father or the Father in Heaven seventy-eight times. It was a term of endearment, a term that spoke volumes about the relationship between Jesus and God.

Good and healthy parental relationships provide children with a strong sense of identity, rock-solid security, and direction in life. Jesus knew he was the child of the one who created heaven and earth. The God of Abraham, Isaac, and Jacob, was his Father. His identity was secure and his purpose in life was fixed—he was the Son of God and he had family business to take care of.

I've always wondered how and when did Jesus become aware of his unique identity as the Son of God? I believe in the incarnation. Jesus was fully divine and fully human. I can get my head around the fully human part, but the fully divine part remains a mystery to me. I wonder if it was a mystery to Jesus?

I suppose Mary and Joseph told him stories about the supernatural activity surrounding his birth. When Jesus was a toddler they probably explained to him, on more than one occasion, why they were living as refugees in Egypt. But when did it dawn on him that he was the unique Son of God?

Because Jesus was fully human, I've always assumed he grew into his identity much like the rest of us. Our family of origin plays a big role in our identity formation, and so did his. Our journey through childhood and the stages of development that lead us from adolescence into adulthood are marked with formative moments. The same must have been true for Jesus. I think the infamous trip to Jerusalem, when Jesus was twelve years old, could have been a formative moment in his life.[5] Routine family trips to the Festival of the Passover, which Mary and Joseph had a custom of attending,

5. Luke 2:4–52.

would have been a family tradition that created warm memories. But when your mom and dad drop the ball and leave you behind in the big city for three days, it becomes more than a memory. Experiences like that have the potential for becoming formative moments in your life. Once Mary and Joseph realized they left Jesus behind, they returned to the city as fast as they could walk. I can hear them arguing with each other as they trudged along the dirt road:

I thought he was with you!

What do you mean, you thought he was with me? I told you to take him with you and the other men.

When they finally found Jesus, he was in the temple, listening to the teachers and asking questions. The boy Jesus was calm and casual about the whole thing. He simply said to his mom and dad: "Why were you searching for me? Didn't you know I had to be in my Father's house?"[6] We're not sure when, nor how Jesus came to realize he was the Son of God, but we do know by the time he was twelve he had a special affinity with God and referred to him as his Father; and he felt at home in the temple.

For many Christians, baptism is a formative moment that molds self-identity. There is no reason to believe the baptism of Jesus was any less formative for him than for us; especially when you consider the descending dove resting on his shoulder and the proclamation from heaven when he came up out of the water. "You are my Son, whom I love; with you I am well pleased."[7]

After his baptism Jesus went on a retreat—fasting, praying, and spending forty days in solitude with God. During the retreat Jesus was tempted, not once, but three times. Each temptation was a direct assault on his identity as the Son of God. Sometimes the tests we endure, the trials we face, and the temptations we overcome help clarify our true identity and the vocational calling on our lives. We can only speculate about how and when Jesus knew himself to be the Son of God; but two things seem obvious to me: when he came out of the wilderness retreat he had a solid and secure

6. Luke 2:49.
7. Mark 1:11.

sense of who he was in relationship to God, and he had a sharp focus on his purpose in life.

For the next three years, Jesus was passionately focused on his vision and mission. He spent every day of his public ministry moving from town to town, preaching and teaching about the kingdom of God. As he moved from place to place he healed the sick, delivered demonized people, and poured his life into the small group of people who traveled with him. Day after day, for three years, Jesus spends his time building friendships with people, teaching his disciples, and loving his neighbors. Woven into this fabric of relationships, like a beautiful tapestry, is his foundational relationship with God. Sometimes we see Jesus slip off early in the morning to pray, other times he spends the evening alone with God. Before making a big decision, like choosing his leadership team, he spends the entire night in prayer. There are moments along the journey when Jesus takes his small group of disciples on personal retreats, to pray and reflect on their experiences. All of his relationships and the work he did revolved around his familial friendship with God.

Because Jesus valued his relationship with God, he had a keen awareness of the mind of God and the movement of God's Spirit. He knew what God was doing and he allowed God's activity to direct his own actions.[8] Jesus listened to the voice of God and knew deep in his own soul what the Spirit of God was saying. Therefore, when Jesus spoke, he said what he heard God saying.[9] In the Gospel of John, when asked to reveal God, Jesus simply said, "Anyone who has seen me has seen the Father."[10] The intimacy shared between Jesus and God provides a window for us to see into the heart and character of God; the things God values are the very things Jesus values, and vice versa. The ways of Jesus are the ways of God.

If our hope is to build a community that looks like Jesus, we will give a great portion of our time and attention to cultivating a spiritual and a deeply intimate friendship with God. Our calendars will have plenty of scheduled appointments where we meet alone with God. We will have a routine where we meet with God in corporate worship. And, we will set apart a portion of time each day to listen intently to God's voice—without distraction. An intimate friendship with God will sharpen our sensitivity to the life and movement of the Holy Spirit in the world. We will become

8. John 5:19; 8:28; 14:31.

9. John 14:10.

10. John 14:9.

more aware that all of life and all relationships are interlaced and lived out in the presence of God. Placing a priority on our friendship with God will increase the value we place on all other relationships; it will increase our capacity to love our family and love our neighbors with higher regard.

Friendship With the Family of God

When you take inventory of the people Jesus shares life with, you see straight away he includes a diverse mix of folks in his inner circle. There are well-to-do tax collectors like Matthew and Zacchaeus, who prior to meeting Jesus very likely made a living by exploiting the poor; there are ordinary, blue-collar fishermen like Peter, James, and John; there's a political zealot named Simon; a thief named Judas; and a weird religious prophet named John, who lived in the wilderness and ate locusts for lunch. Women are a part of his inner circle of friends. They traveled with Jesus from the beginning of his public ministry and supported him out of their own means. Jesus has late-night conversations with well-respected and highly educated community leaders like Nicodemus and he shares drinks and dinner parties with sinners and lepers. Jesus gets called out and criticized more than once for keeping company with such a mix of unclean and unacceptable people. But the criticism fell on deaf ears. The rebuke of the religious leaders did not alter his values one iota. Jesus valued people, all people regardless of their social class, religious persuasion, or ethnicity. Jesus loves diversity; it's obvious by his actions. He crossed over major social and religious barriers to invite a diverse group of people into his circle of friends; a circle he considered family.

On one occasion Jesus and his disciples were staying at a friend's house, trying to get some rest and a bite to eat, when all of a sudden a crowd of folks show up to hear him preach and watch him perform a miracle or two. His mom shows up at the party, along with his brothers. The Scripture says they came to "take charge of him,"[11] which is a polite way of saying they thought he had lost his ever-loving mind. Reports were coming in regarding the company Jesus was keeping, the things he was teaching, and the miracles he was performing. Some were beginning to accuse Jesus of being demon-possessed and his kinfolk were either embarrassed or concerned that it might be true. When they arrived at the place where Jesus was teaching they stood outside and requested to speak with him.

11. Mark 3:21.

I can see Jesus roll his eyes with a "here-we-go-again" sigh. This time he used the opportunity as an object lesson to teach every one in the room, as well as his mom who was standing outside, about the family of God. He looked at those seated in the circle around him and said, "Here are my mother and my brothers! Whoever does God's will is my brother and sister and mother."[12] Jesus stretched the branches of the family tree beyond bloodline and beyond nationality. According to Jesus, the family of God includes any and all who do the will of God.

The people sitting in the circle that day represented a cross section of every social, political, or economic spectrum you can imagine. These people would have never kept company with one another, nor met together under the same roof, if not for Jesus. The same is true for his smaller band of disciples. The handful of men and women who followed him as he traveled back and forth across Judea wouldn't have been caught in the same room together for a day, let alone spent three years working side by side, helping Jesus build a beloved community. The value Jesus placed on the family of God and his deep desire for unity within the family impacted the atmosphere around him and created a culture where people wanted to be together, not in spite of their differences, but because of their commonality in Christ.

Richard Twiss, author of *One Church, Many Tribes,* once said, "you cannot have unity in the absence of diversity."[13] Twiss asserts that unity void of diversity is nothing more than conformity. I would suggest this is one reason Jesus infused diversity into his circle of friends. Unfortunately, much of what we consider as unity in church culture today is glorified conformity. Homogenous groups of people who think alike, look alike, dress, vote, sing, and dance alike, and act nice to each other on Sunday morning are not the model of unity Jesus had in mind for the family of God. This kind of conformity is easy to pull off, but it lacks luster. It is void of power and offers no witness to the world regarding God's beautiful design for creation and God's intention for the family of God.

It is God's desire for people to live in peace and solidarity with one another. Diversity and unity in the family of God is to be a blessing and a witness to the rest of the world. Jesus flipped over tables in the temple because the moneychangers were frustrating this fundamental intention of God. Jesus scolded the scam artist for turning God's house of prayer into a

---

12. Mark 3:20–34.

13. Twiss, "CCDA National Conference 2011," 53:46–53:50.

marketplace. Their moneymaking enterprise was preventing gentiles, people of other nations, from having a place to pray in the temple. With whip in hand, Jesus quotes the prophet Isaiah and says, "My house will be called a house of prayer for all nations. But you have made it a den of robbers."[14] Two things grab my attention when I read this story. One, Jesus has a burning passion for prayer. The temple was created to be a house of prayer, a place where people could experience intimate friendship with God. Two, Jesus expects all nations to be included and welcome in the house, not as foreigners to be exploited, but as family.

God loves diversity. The variety of color, culture, and language scattered across the globe is a reflection of God's creativity and beauty. The fact that every cheetah spot, zebra stripe, and human fingerprint from the beginning of time is a unique original screams to me: "God detests sameness!"[15] In the book of Revelation we get a glimpse into heaven through the eyes of John. The people gathered around the throne of God are a grand display of diversity. John is invited by an angel to peek into heaven and he tells us what he saw. "I looked, and there before me was a great multitude that no one could count, from every nation, tribe, people, and language, standing before the throne and before the Lamb."[16] God's family is a diverse and messy mix of people from every tribe and every nation.

When Jesus built his community of disciples, he did it with diversity in mind. He created a microcosmic community that would bear witness to the world as to what heaven on earth would look like. His family was a group of diverse people and he wanted them to live in solidarity with one another. It wasn't a suggestion on his part—he insisted that brothers and sisters in his family love one another, and he prayed for us to experience the same level of unity that he experienced with God.[17]

In John 13, Jesus gave his disciples a new command, a command to love one another. His instruction went far beyond a sappy Hallmark card platitude or a Beatles song; it was a command to love one another in the same way Jesus had loved them. Jesus told his disciples, "As I have loved you, so you must love one another. By this everyone will know that you are my disciples, if you love one another."[18] Jesus valued the family of God. His

14. Mark 11:17.

15. Yaconelli, *Messy Spirituality*, 103–5.

16. Rev 7:9.

17. John 17:20–23.

18. John 13:35.

hope and prayer was for us to love one another with the depth of love he modeled, and to live in solidarity with one another.

We cannot sidestep this core value and consider ourselves the family of God or followers of Jesus. A community based on the values of Jesus will desire diversity, and it will make every effort to live in unity. Loving one another in the manner that Jesus loved us will be the standard by which we evaluate our community life. That's a tall order and a very lofty goal. I take comfort in our community, knowing Jesus prayed for his original disciples and for those who would follow him because of their witness. He prayed that we would love one another and live in unity. He wants us to be one, as he and God are one. Moving towards that goal is a step towards the intention of Jesus for the family of God on earth.

Loving one another and living in unity with the family of God gives us the fortitude and the capacity we need to love our neighbors. When a diverse community is united in Christ and inspired by his love, they will have a deep desire to befriend the poor and to love those who are overlooked by the systems of this world.

Friendship with the Forgotten

You cannot embrace the values of Jesus and neglect to embrace the poor. A friend of Jesus will befriend the oppressed. As we watch Jesus engage in relationships with the poor, we get a glimpse at how he moves in rhythm with God's heart. Friendship with the poor and the forgotten comes natural to Jesus, as natural as breathing. You never see him patronize or exploit people. He never forces his agenda on them. Compassion and love are always his motivation, never pity. When you listen in on the conversations Jesus has with people, you get a strong sense that he loves everyone he meets; and yet, he seems to have a special affinity with those who are poor and marginalized.

When I first began reading the Bible, one of the things that attracted me to Jesus was the way he showed partiality toward the poor. I was fascinated by how he favored the social outcasts and sinners over religious leaders. I thought that was amazing . . . until I became a religious leader. As a white religious leader with a middle-class income, his "preference for the poor" became a little disconcerting on a personal level. I began to identify with and wonder if Matthew, a former tax collector who probably accumulated some wealth before meeting Jesus, might have tweaked the Beatitude as recorded in the Gospel of Luke. Luke quotes Jesus saying, "Blessed are the poor"; Matthew says, "Blessed are the poor in spirit."[19] Sometimes I wonder if Matthew spiritualized the text because he was rich.

Maybe? Or maybe it's God's way of letting us know that everyone matters. It is evident in Scripture; everyone—despite their social position, economic status, race, ethnicity, gender, or sexual orientation—has a special place in God's heart and a shared need for grace and mercy. With that being said, it is equally apparent in the Bible that God gives special attention to those who are poor and oppressed by the systems and principalities of the world. More than 2,000 verses are woven into the pages of the Bible verifying God's special concern for the poor. The prophetic literature condemns imperialistic systems and individuals who abuse their power and build wealth on the backs of disenfranchised people.[20] Jesus taught about God's concern for the poor[21] and demonstrated God's concern by loving his neighbors who were beleaguered and forgotten.[22]

A community built around the values of Jesus will emulate his concern for the poor. They will proclaim with word and deed that everyone matters! And because everyone matters, they will give special attention to the poor, speak out on behalf of those who are oppressed, and seek ways to create a world where no one is treated as if their life doesn't matter.

As I write these words, our city and hundreds of other cities around the world are grieving with demonstrations of outrage and protest in response to the killings of Breonna Taylor, George Floyd, and Ahmaud Arbery.[23] Years of unheard complaint that the criminal justice system in the United States of America discriminates against people of color have reached a breaking point. The unjustifiable death of these three individuals has motivated thousands of people to take to the streets and speak out against the status quo of injustice—an injustice that has its roots deeply embedded in a culture of white supremacy.

This diverse mix of people, from all walks of life and every corner of the globe, are standing in solidarity with our black and brown neighbors.

---

19. Luke 6:20; Matt 5:3.

20. Isa 3:14–15; 10:1–2; Ezek 22:11–13; Amos 5:10–12; 8:4–6; Zech 7:9–11.

21. Luke 4:18–19; 6:20–26; 14:7–14; 16:19–31; Matt 25:31–46.

22. Matt 11:1–6; Luke 8:43–48; John 8:1–11.

23. At the time of this writing, 589 cities and towns in the United States, representing all fifty states and sixty-nine cities globally, have held some form of public demonstration or protest in response to these three tragic events and years of racial injustice.

They are speaking up and speaking out, adding their tears to the lament and their voice to the complaint. Their message is clear: black lives matter! Everyone, regardless of the color of their skin, should be treated with reverence and equitable regard.

I lift up this moment in American history as an example for two reasons. One, Ms. Taylor was a resident of Louisville, a neighbor of mine whose death has rocked our city to the core. How our city responds and how the church does or does not add its voice to the cry for justice will mold the future of America—for better, or for worse. Second, in times such as these, Christian communities have the opportunity and the responsibility to demonstrate the values of Jesus. Now is the time for the church to show up with our brothers and sisters who have been harmed and exploited by centuries of racism, and say, "Enough is enough!"

In the wake of Ms. Taylor's death, millions of people have added their voices and their opinions to the conversation regarding racial injustice. Some of the voices have been extremely helpful—others, not so much. Some have said dreadful things, bringing insult to injury; while others remain silent, which says more than one might imagine. A community built on the values of Jesus will not remain silent in the face of social injustice.

One of the quotes I read this week that captured my attention was from Parker Palmer, the author of *On the Brink of Everything*. Palmer says, "I urge those of you who cling to your dream of the 'good old days'—good for you, anyway—to take a nice long nap and dream on, dream on. The rest of us will stay awake and help midwife the rebirth of America, hoping that our national nausea in this moment is just another symptom that our country is pregnant with change."[24]

Is it possible that our country is finally at a place where we're ready and willing to deal with our original sin of racism? Are we ready to work together, to dismantle racialized policies and procedures that keep some people living on the margins, poor, and frustrated, while others flourish? Are we ready to give birth to a culture that does not favor one group of people over another?

Yes, our country is pregnant with possibility. We have the opportunity to give birth to a new America where everyone matters, where every family has the opportunity to flourish, and every person enjoys the same Constitutional freedoms as everyone else. I believe this new world is possible. To get there, communities that follow the way of Jesus must show up and add

24. Palmer, *On the Brink*, 137.

their voices to the cause. People in positions of power and privilege must join the conversation and push for radical change. We must stay awake and stay engaged in the conversation. And by all means, we must quit dreaming about the good old days, which were good for some and horrific for others. We can no longer settle for a world where some people are forgotten and treated as if their lives don't matter.

A community built around the values of Jesus will embrace God's concern for the least of these. We will show up at the public square and add our voice to support the cause of racial righteousness and social justice. Concern for the poor, the oppressed, and the forgotten is a value of Jesus. A community built on his values will imitate his concern. In the words of Ron Sider, author of *Just Generosity,* "If we do not imitate God's concern for the poor we are not really God's people—no matter how frequent our worship or how orthodox our creeds."[25]

The primary core value for Jesus was love. Love for God and love for people. This value was his central organizing principle for life and he worked it out through the friendships he made—friendship with God, friendship with the family of God, and friendship with the forgotten. If we want to organize our community around the values of Jesus, love and friendship will be our primary organizing principles.

Fire

The love Jesus had for God and the love he had for people was not the casual, take-it-or-leave-it, I-just-want-to-feel-good brand of love we see in most church congregations today. On the contrary, the love demonstrated in the life and death of Jesus was far more passionate. When I read the Gospels and observe how Jesus lived and died, when I watch how he demonstrated his love for God and his concern for the people of God, and when I take note of the bold stands he made for the people who were pushed to the margins of life, I see a red-hot, fiery passion, the kind of passion that needs yellow caution tape surrounding it to keep people who don't want to be consumed by his passion at a safe distance.

It was my friend Tattoo Johnny who helped me realize the importance of keeping the three relationship networks of Jesus in balance with one

25. Sider, *Just Generosity,* 58.

another. We had three Johns on our church planting leadership team: First John, Second John, and Third John. Calling them First, Second, and Third John was funny at first, but no one could remember who was who. It was a *revelation* for us all when we discovered a new name for Third John.

First John had been around the longest; hence the honor of being called First John. Second John rolled into town a couple years later. Chronologically speaking, it made sense for him to be dubbed Second John. Prior to locating in Portland, Second John was living in his mini van, zigzagging across the United States, working on a PhD in Christian leadership. His style of leadership reminded me of Moses, who spent forty years zigzagging through the wilderness before entering the promised land. Like Moses, Second John wandered around aimlessly from city to city, sleeping in his mini van and attending classes on the Internet before he finally discovered Portland.

Finally, there was Third John (aka Tattoo Johnny), who had the coolest tattoos in the neighborhood—which represents a lot of tattoos. His left forearm was covered with blue waves of rushing water. The color and the detail of the tattoo made it look like he just got out of the shower and needed a towel to dry off. His right forearm was covered with red and orange flames—the kind of flames you see painted on the side of race cars. When I asked him about his tattoos, he lifted both arms in the air and said, "These tats remind me that I have been baptized by water and fire!" And then he pushed his shoulder length, salt-and-pepper hair out of his face, cocked his head a little to the right, and said with a sly grin, "You know what I mean?"

Tattoo Johnny had been praying with us on Sunday mornings and attending our Celebrate Recovery program for almost two years. When I asked him to be part of our leadership team he asked me, "What kind of church are we anyway? Are we nondenominational or what?" I smiled and said, "It doesn't really matter that much, but if someone important asks, we are United Methodist!" We laughed and then he slapped me on the back and said, "I know what you mean!"

When our leadership team began meeting, the big question we had to answer was: "What kind of United Methodist Church were we going to be?" The first step in answering the question was to discern the values of Jesus. We wanted the things that were important to him to be important to us. We identified the three relational networks of Jesus and agreed that loving God, loving the family of God, and loving our marginalized neighbors would be the primary focus of our community. These would be the friendships that mattered the most and we would do everything we could to inspire passion in all three areas. This is how we talk about the three friendship networks at Church of the Promise:

- We want to *Know* God wholeheartedly.
- We want to *Grow* a community that lives and loves like Jesus.
- We want to *Go* to the streets and share the love of Christ.

One day when we were praying together, trying to dive deep into what it might look like for us to set these three friendship networks in the center of all we do, Tattoo Johnny had a "word to share." That's how he liked to pray. He would interrupt the flow of the prayer and begin to talk to everyone in the room. He would start by saying: "I have a word to share . . . I think God is saying . . ." and then Tattoo Johnny would lay a prophetic zinger on us. Sometimes, what he had to say was just weird and quickly dismissed. But other times the word was right on point and shifted everything.

On this particular day he said, "I think the three friendship circles of Jesus are like the three elements you need to build a fire. A fire needs oxygen, fuel, and heat in order to burn; if one of them is missing, the fire goes out. But when you get all three together, the fire burns bright. If we focus on all three of these friendships at the same time, with the same level of gusto for each, we will have a Holy Ghost Bonfire!" And then he flipped his hair, smiled, and said, "You know what I mean?"

The word made sense and it spoke to me at a deep level. Over the years of following Jesus, I've noticed that local congregations have a tendency to focus on one or two of these relationship networks, but few give equal passion and attention to all three at the same time.[26] Pentecostal brothers and sisters have a burning passion for experiencing God through worship and prayer, while evangelical churches have a tendency to focus the weight of their attention on personal salvation and helping people grow deep in their knowledge of Scripture. These two streams focus on friendship with God and friendship with the family of God. The third relationship network, friendship with the forgotten, captures the attention of the progressive streams in our church family.

When it comes to personal holiness and social holiness, it seems that congregations tend to prefer one or the other, even when they say both are important. For the life of me, I have never understood why passion for one

26. Breen, *Building a Discipling Culture*, 83–85.

relationship network doesn't drive us to desire the other on deeper levels. The more I get to know Jesus through encounters with the Holy Spirit, the more my heart breaks for the things that break God's heart. The more I read Scripture, the more I'm driven to love both God and neighbor. The longer I stand with others to resist social evil and organize groups to pursue social holiness, the more I'm driven to my knees to seek the mercy and presence of God.

Tattoo Johnny was right; we need equal passion in all three relationships. We need the life-giving oxygen that comes from our friendship with God. We need passionate worship and spiritual disciplines that help us encounter God's Holy Spirit in deep and personal ways. We need the fuel that comes through our friendship with the family of God—relationships and opportunities that challenge us to know and apply Scripture, so we can learn how to live and love like Jesus. And, we need the heat that comes when we pursue social justice. We need creative ways to stand in solidarity with the poor and the prophetic imagination to stand against social evil in whatever forms it presents itself. If we remove one element from the equation, the fire will burn out. A little of one element added to an abundant supply of the other two will keep the fire burning, but the fire will cast a dim light. If we place equal passion and focused attention on all three relationships, the fire will burn hot and bright.

With Tattoo Johnny's help, we finally decided what kind of United Methodist Church we wanted to be—a beloved community that burns bright with the red-hot, fiery passion of Jesus! Loving God with all of our heart, soul, mind, and strength; loving the family of God in the same way Jesus loves us; and loving those who are forgotten with the relentless, audacious love of Christ.

There's a myth that floats around on the Internet, suggesting that John Wesley told the people called Methodists to "light yourself on fire with passion and people will come from miles to watch you burn." Even though Wesley never said it, that's the kind of church we want to be—a church where love and friendship with God and neighbor burns like a Holy Ghost Bonfire . . . You know what I mean?

RED LETTER QUESTIONS

Do you truly love me more than these?

1. In John 21:15–19, Jesus takes a walk on the beach with Simon Peter. While they stroll along, kicking sand from their sandals, Jesus asks Peter the same question three times, *"Do you love me?"* Why do you think Jesus asks the question multiple times?

2. The first time he poses the question he specifically asks: *"Simon, son of John, do you truly love me more than these?"* This is a values clarification question. What do you think Jesus was referring to when he said, *"more than these?"*

3. If Jesus were walking with you or your community, what would he point to if he were to ask, *"Do you truly love me more than these?"*

4. Take some time and evaluate where you and/or your community invests the majority of your time and financial resources. After the assessment, would you conclude that your core values align with the core values of Jesus discussed in this chapter?

5. The number-one core value of Jesus is love for God and love for people. We saw in the chapter how Jesus focused his life and resources on three friendship networks. Most faith communities will champion one or two of the friendship networks but find it difficult to focus equal attention on all three. How do you and/or your community focus time and resources on the three friendship networks?

   • Friendship with God?

   • Friendship with the Family of God?

   • Friendship with the Forgotten?

6. Is there balance between the three relational networks in your community or does one network outweigh the others?

2

Downward Mobility

"The way of Jesus is not the way of upward mobility in which our world has invested so much, but the way of downward mobility ending on the cross."

HENRI NOUWEN

"The Son of Man did not come to be served, but to serve, and to give his life as a ransom for many."

JESUS

FRIENDSHIP HAS A WAY of bringing out the best in us, because true friendship will seek to give its best and will desire what is best for the friend. When we follow the way of Jesus, and make friendship with God, friendship with the family of God, and friendship with those who are forgotten—our core values—it will inspire us to be more intentional about how we share life with our neighbors. The core value of love and friendship motivated Jesus to live a downwardly mobile life, a concept articulated by the twentieth-century contemplative author Henri Nouwen.

The Descending Way of Jesus

In his book *Here and Now,* Nouwen contrasts the world's value of upward mobility to the "descending way of Jesus." He writes, "In a society in which upward mobility is the norm, downward mobility is not only discouraged but even considered unwise, unhealthy, or downright stupid."[1] To highlight the absurdity of downward mobility, Nouwen raises a series of questions:

- Who will freely choose a low-paying job when a high-paying job is being offered?

- Who will choose poverty when wealth is within reach?

- Who will choose the hidden place when there is a place in the limelight?

- Who will choose to be with one person in great need when many people could be helped during the same time?[2]

There are fundamental narratives in our culture that support and encourage upward mobility. The great American Dream, the pursuit of personal happiness as an unalienable right, rugged individualism, a capitalistic economy driven by consumerism, and the subtle influence of Darwinian theory that champions the survival of the fittest, are sub-narratives in our culture that reinforce the value of upward mobility. In the face of these narratives, downward mobility is both counterintuitive and countercultural. But it is the way of Jesus. Nouwen says those who choose to follow the descending way of Jesus will discover it is the way that leads toward the poor.[3] When we take Jesus seriously and adopt downward mobility as a value, it will greatly influence our decisions and reorient the trajectory of our lives. There may be occasions along the way when we question the wisdom of those decisions.

Peter had one of those moments when he questioned the sacrifice he made to follow Jesus and wondered if it would pay off in the end. It was on the heels of a conversation between Jesus and a man of great wealth, who asked Jesus what he must do to gain eternal life. Jesus and the rich man had a challenging conversation as Peter listened in. They talked about the meaning of goodness and mused about the law. Then Jesus told the man he lacked one thing. He needed to shift his values from upward mobility to a life of sacrifice. Jesus challenged the man to free himself from the idolatrous grip of affluence and invited him on an extraordinary adventure. "Go sell everything you have and give to the poor, and you will have treasure in

1. Nouwen, *Here and Now,* 100.

2. Nouwen, *Here and Now,* 100.

3. Nouwen, *Here and Now,* 101.

heaven. Then come, follow me."[4] The Bible tells us the man became very sad because he had a lot of wealth. After the rich man walks away, Peter pipes up and says, "We have left all we had to follow you!" In the context, Peter's comment seems more like a question than a statement. "We've left everything . . . is it enough?" Jesus responds to Peter by saying, "Truly I tell you no one who has left home or wife or brothers or sisters or parents or children for the sake of the kingdom of God will fail to receive many times as much in this age, and in the age to come eternal life."[5]

Downward mobility may not be the way of the world, nor the predominant narrative in the church, but it is the way of Jesus. Communities built around the values of Jesus will have a bent towards downward mobility. And, according to Jesus, the reward for following his descending way will outweigh the rewards upward mobility offers, both in this world and in the world to come. Following Jesus is a journey filled with eternal treasures wrapped up in the people we meet and the friendships we make along the way.

The Great *Awokening*

When Kathie and I first married we dreamed about living in a log cabin, overlooking a lake in the middle of the country. You can imagine how surprised we were to find ourselves living in an urban context. We were equally surprised by two other facts. One, how unprepared we were for urban life. Two, how "unwoke" we were in regards to our white privilege and the value we placed on upward mobility. It was my new friend Chris who helped me come to terms with my unconscious bias in both regards.

Chris was a teenager in our program. I'll never forget the day he read our fundraising brochure. It was one of those "pimping poverty" brochures, filled with pictures of poor kids and heart-wrenching descriptions of the neighborhood. The purpose of the marketing piece was to motivate rich people to give a lot of money. I hate to admit it, but this particular brochure was one of the worst I've ever seen—before or since. We used stock photos of poor kids because our children didn't look sad enough to trouble the hearts of rich people. Chris slowly read the brochure and then tossed it on the floor. He looked me square in the eye and said, "Larry, we were fine long before you got here and we'll be fine long after you're gone."

4. Luke 18:22.
5. Luke 18:29.

That's the day I began to wake up and realize how sick and twisted my perspective on mission and ministry was. Before my friend Chris confronted me with a sobering dose of truth, my unspoken agenda had been to help the kids in the neighborhood meet Jesus, get a quality education, land a good-paying job, and then move up and out of Portland to a "nice neighborhood" like mine. I'm embarrassed now to even write it; but we all start from somewhere, right? My somewhere just happened to be white, middle-class, conservative, and suburban. It was a place of privilege.

Chris no longer lives in Portland, but we chat on Facebook now and then. From time to time, he will post something about leaving me behind in the neighborhood—along with an LOL—reminding me of the hard conversation we had way back when. It was a hard conversation, but it helped me realize there was much I needed to learn and equally as much, if not more, that I needed to unlearn. The first item on the unlearning curve was to rethink my motives and to embrace the value of downward mobility.

I soon came to understand that our culture's obsession with upward mobility was a primary factor contributing to the disinvestment in urban neighborhoods. There are huge economic implications when people with social, political, and financial wherewithal move up and out of neighborhoods. Retail stores, small businesses, economic investors, and jobs, as well as the church, follow the migration. Upward mobility will leave behind a disenfranchised neighborhood, with an economic and a leadership vacuum.[6]

After the "Great Awokening" I began to listen with new ears and a new posture. I was eager to listen and learn. The teenagers we worked with had delightful stories of growing up together in Portland. They told funny stories of childhood adventures. They joked on each other nonstop, laughing louder and louder as the stories unfolded. I listened to their parents as they shared their versions of the same stories.

The two perspectives were always quite different. As we sat around on car hoods or on front porch swings, I listened to their memories of days gone by. Woven into the narrative, like a subplot in a well-written play, was a theme of pride and a hope for the future. They loved the neighborhood. It was home, and they didn't want to move out, but they did dream about making their neighborhood better.

Kathie and I began to seriously discuss the importance of relocating our family to the neighborhood where God had us in ministry. If we were

6. Perkins, *Beyond Charity*, 72–73.

going to faithfully serve our neighbors as a family on mission, we actually needed to be neighbors. Their hopes and dreams for the neighborhood needed to become our hopes and dreams. The concerns and social problems our new friends were facing needed to become our problems as well. We needed to share life together so we could move from saying "them" and "they" to saying "we" and "us." The value of friendship and the value of downward mobility were weighing on us and prompting us to move. We wanted to live and work side by side with our new friends, loving "our" neighborhood together.

The decision to relocate our family to Portland was not one we made in haste. We took some time to discern God's timing and to clarify our motives. We knew the move would not turn out well if the motive was to relieve the guilt my friend Chris provoked. On the other hand, it was becoming obvious that the relationships we longed to establish would be extremely limited if we chose to live on the other side of town.

The longer we pondered the question, the clearer the answer became. We really did want to share life and create meaningful stories with the families in Portland. We wanted to be present in their lives, during the simple, ordinary rhythms of life, including sacred celebrations, as well as the stress-filled challenges. We wanted to be present in their lives and share proximity with them. And, we wanted our new friends to have access to our lives as well. That's the way intentional neighboring works.

Incarnational Living

After we moved to the city, I soon discovered incarnational living is far more involved than simply changing your address. Trust and credibility with neighbors is not established just because you live next door to one another. It takes time and a good measure of intentional neighboring. I may be overstating the obvious, but if you want to gain trust and credibility with your neighbor, you have to be trustworthy and credible.

I have a friend who was a CEO of an international corporation based here in Louisville. He once told me if you want to be a good leader, the people you lead must know you really care about them and they must be convinced you have their best interest at heart; and then he asked me if I knew how to convince people you really care. When I inquired how, he said: "You really care!"

Living an incarnational life with the hope of expressing God's love and concern for people is similar. You must really care. You must really have your neighbor's best interest at heart. In order to live out an incarnational life that represents the kingdom of God, you must love your neighbor in ways that are congruent with the nature and character of Jesus.

Alan Hirsch, missional church leader and author of *Forgotten Ways*, identifies four characteristics in the incarnation of Jesus that will benefit those who desire to connect with neighbors in a way that truly honors them: the ministry of presence, intentional proximity, relinquishing power, and finally, a transparent and humble proclamation of the gospel.[7] Practicing these four elements, expressed in the incarnation of Christ, will add credibility and authenticity to the person who chooses to follow the descending way of Jesus.

Presence and Proximity

When we choose to follow the way of Jesus and live in proximity with marginalized people, we help cultivate a context for the grace and mercy of God to be experienced through natural, organic friendships. Let's take a moment and consider the ministry of presence in relation to intentional proximity. They are two sides of the same coin. Sharing geographical space does not guarantee you will be present with those you are proximate with. You can live next door to someone and choose not to be present in their life. In our fast-paced, individualistic culture, it is far too easy to neglect the opportunities we have to know and love our neighbors. When Kathie and I lived in the suburbs, we owned a small ranch house that sat on an acre of land. After we lived there a couple of years, my cousin moved into the ranch house next door. Our families lived side by side for several years, yet we never took the time to be present in one another's life. In the heat of the summer when the grass was green and tall we would drive around the property on our riding mowers and send a courteous wave across the fence, but we never took the time or made the effort to be present with one another. How easy and refreshing it would have been to turn off the mowers and have a chat across the fence. If you want to live an incarnational life for the sake of the gospel, you must be aware of your social interactions, take opportunities to engage in conversations with your neighbors, and pay attention to the ministry of presence.

7. Hirsch, *Forgotten Ways*, 131–34.

The ministry of presence is a spiritual discipline that trains our soul to be fully present with another person. It is good to know your neighbors by name and take the time to visit and talk with one another. It is a great step in the right direction. Unfortunately, we can engage in a conversation with another person and still fall extremely short of being present in the moment with them. The ministry of presence takes ordinary conversations and seizes the moment to build authentic friendship, trust, and credibility.

The Ministry of Presence

Being vulnerable by making yourself emotionally and physically available to others is risky business, yet it is a prerequisite for anyone who desires to build meaningful friendships and connect spiritually with others. "Vulnerability," according to Brené Brown, author of *Daring Greatly*, "is the core, the heart, the center, of meaningful human experiences."[8] Learning how to listen to others, learning how to focus on the moment, learning how to be truly present, and having the emotional guts to risk inviting others into your personal life is an ongoing spiritual exercise for the human soul. Incarnational ministry, Jesus-style, is vulnerable and packed to the brim with risk. Remember, his choice to be downwardly mobile, present, and vulnerable cost him his life.

Jesus listened to others, he knew the heart and the intentions of people, and he was well aware of the social and political systems that elevated some people and oppressed others. When he spoke, he spoke words of encouragement, as well as words of prophetic truth. I believe his willingness to be fully present with others and fully present with God simultaneously gave Jesus the capacity to incarnate the kingdom of heaven while on earth. Jesus had a way of listening to the Holy Spirit as he engaged deeply in conversations with others. I'm certain that's why Jesus paused before responding to the Pharisees' questions about what to do with the woman caught in adultery. Anxiety was high, a woman's life was on the line, and the men in power with judicial authority were pressing Jesus for an answer: "What do you say? Shall we stone her or not?" How does Jesus respond? He stoops down and doodles in the dirt. He is a non-anxious presence in the midst of chaos and drama, with the ability to listen to the Holy Spirit and then speak

8. Brown, *Daring Greatly*, 12.

prophetically into the moment. When he stands up he simply says, "Let any one of you who is without sin be the first to throw a stone at her."[9]

When we stretch ourselves to imitate the incarnational lifestyle of Jesus we will learn how to engage more fully in holy conversations. Like Jesus, humility and honor will be the posture we take as we listen to our neighbors with both ears, while our inner ear listens to the voice of God's Spirit. If we delight in the stories our neighbors tell, God will add depth and substance to our own story. The level of vulnerability we are willing to assume will determine the gravity and authenticity of the friendships we build. As we learn how to be fully present with other people and with God simultaneously, we increase the potential for spiritual discernment and prophetic encouragement to flow into our conversations. The Holy Spirit will prompt us with words of encouragement to speak and relevant questions to ask. The level of trust will grow deeper and the conversations we share will lead the friendship into sacred space.

Proximity

The ministry of presence is the discipline of being fully engaged in the moment—however routine and mundane it is—with a desire to honor the life of others who are in the moment with us. The ministry of proximity is the decision we make that determines whom we will share the moments of life with. The amazing truth of the incarnation is the profound fact that God chose to come close to Earth and spend time with people. While on Earth, in the person of Jesus, God became proximate with the poor and the wealthy, with religious leaders and tax collectors, with political leaders and social outcasts, with saints and sinners. Through Christ, God became accessible and available. When we become proximate with the poor, we not only increase the opportunity of being present in their lives, we create the opportunity for them to have access to ours.

Incarnational proximity creates sacred space where we are both host and guest; we are the one who extends hospitality and at the same time receives the gift of hospitality from others. We give and receive, lend and borrow, teach and learn as we walk out the rhythms of life and enjoy spontaneous moments with our neighbors. Genuine, godly friendships lived out in the normal flow of life is one sign the kingdom of heaven has come near to Earth.

9. John 8:7.

In her book, *The Power of Proximity*, Michelle Ferrigno Warren says, "A life of proximity to the poor is powerful because its story cannot be wrapped up in one small individual package; it is a collective, faith-filled life lived day after day alongside the pain and suffering of others. We do not simply desire the elimination of pain but a renewed spirit and refined heart as we share it together."[10]

The way God chose to redeem pain and address the brokenness caused by sin was to become proximate with it. God left heaven and moved into the neighborhood on purpose. Following the way of Christ will compel us with a burden to see that which is broken in our world made right, and for those who are harmed by the brokenness made whole. Warren says, "The most profound move you can make to address pain and injustice is to become proximate to it . . . Becoming proximate to the poor, those impacted most by injustice, is the most radical, transformative thing you can do to affect it."[11]

Powerlessness and Proclamation

If we value downward mobility and desire to live an incarnational life that looks like Jesus, the value will have implications on how we exercise power and how we proclaim the gospel. *Humble* and *meek* are two words that come to mind as I think about how Jesus related with people while visiting the planet. He did not lord his power over people, nor did he leverage his privilege as the Son of God to gratify self-interest. In other words, Jesus didn't force his agenda on people. He didn't coerce people to respond in a prescribed way to the message he presented. On the contrary, he laid aside his power in order to live in solidarity with humanity.

In his letter to the Philippian church, the apostle Paul offers a beautiful description of the descending way of Jesus and exhorts those who profess faith in Christ to follow his example: "Our attitude should be the same as that of Christ Jesus: Who being in very nature God, did not consider equality with God something to be grasped but made himself nothing, taking the very nature of a servant, being made in human likeness. And being found in appearance as a man, he humbled himself and became obedient to death—even death on a cross."[12] It blows me away to reflect on this truth:

10. Warren, *Power of Proximity*, 162.

11. Warren, *Power of Proximity*, 7–8.

12. Phil 2:6–7.

when Almighty God, creator of heaven and earth, decided to live an incarnational life among us, God set power and privilege aside. In so doing, Jesus revealed the humble nature and self-giving character of God. Therefore, if we value downward mobility and choose to live in a Christlike way, we will not rely on normal forms of power, exploit our position, or make grand assumptions about our privilege, in order to proclaim the gospel. We must observe the Jesus model presented in Philippians and take it with absolute seriousness.

Alan Hirsch points out that Jesus is quite explicit about this and reminds his reader of the time when Jesus instructed his friends on how they were to use their power and how they were to leverage their position as apostolic leaders:[13] "Jesus called them together and said, 'You know that the rulers of the Gentiles lord it over them, and their high officials exercise authority over them. Not so with you. Instead, whoever wants to become great among you must be your servant, and whoever wants to be first must be your slave just as the Son of Man did not come to be served, but to serve, and to give his life as a ransom for many."[14]

A cursory look at church history will reveal how often we have failed to live out and proclaim the gospel in a Christlike way. It is sad and difficult to acknowledge how little we have assimilated this humble-servant aspect of incarnational Christlikeness into our understanding of church leadership and mission.[15] Eurocentric Christendom, during the Crusades, as well as more recent models of mission expansion—sometimes naïve and innocent, other times not so naïve—abused power to promote self-interest and/or national interest in the name of Christ or the church.

Even when we take exploitation out of the equation and assume the most altruistic motive when proclaiming the gospel of Christ, it is difficult for people in positions of power and privilege to set aside their power in order to simply stand in solidarity with those who are poor and marginalized. Hidden within our desire to help and fix what we think is broken, or to be victorious when faced with a challenge, is a subtle temptation to assert our power and become the hero in an epic story. Because of this subtle temptation, we have failed on many occasions to approach our mission with humility and Christlike meekness.

13. Hirsch, *Forgotten Ways*, 134.

14. Matt 20:25–28.

15. Hirsch, *Forgotten Ways*, 134.

Downward mobility and incarnation is the radical way God chose to relate to people, to reveal the nature and character of God, and to make a way for the salvation of the world.[16] When Jesus came to Earth, he did not come with coercive power but with genuine humility. He became poor and stood in solidarity with the poor. He emptied himself and befriended those on the margins of society. He became a servant and through his obedience unto death made a way for people to experience the true nature and character of God's heart. From this humble position, God was able to lift up all of humanity; and through Christ, God created a way for mortal humans to be seated with Christ at the right hand of God in the heavenly realms.[17] That's cool news! It's more than cool; it is a powerful story of good news that deserves to be proclaimed. And, I would add, all people from every walk of life, every tribe, nation, and language, deserve to hear it.

Proclaiming this good news to the world is woven into the missional call of the church. We cannot ignore our commission to proclaim God's love for the world, which was demonstrated through the incarnation of Jesus, and remain faithful to our calling.[18] However, when we do proclaim this good news, we must proclaim it in a way that honors Jesus; we must emulate his humility and his meekness. Downward mobility and incarnational living are values of Jesus. If we embrace these values it will greatly impact the way we express God's love and share God's story.

Dinner Time

Let's consider some of the ways Jesus proclaimed the gospel and expressed God's love and friendship for people through downward mobility and incarnational living. A friend of mine once said, "Jesus came to save the world and he did it by eating and drinking." That's a brilliant saying, and for all practical purposes it rings true. Jesus knew how to have a good time with his friends, and apparently he was a foodie. Everywhere you turn in the gospel stories, Jesus is sharing a meal with someone. He came to Earth to proclaim good news of great joy and he did it over the dinner table, or at parties, or some festive occasion, like a wedding feast.

Remember the wedding party where they ran out of wine and his mother prompted him to make more so the party could go on? My friend

16. Hirsch and Frost, *Shaping of Things*, 35–40.
17. Eph 2:4–7.
18. Hirsch, *Forgotten Ways*, 134.

Jared likes to point out that they didn't run out of wine until Jesus and his friends showed up . . . Hmm? The apostle John calls the miracle a sign. I think it's a sign that Jesus likes parties and having a good time with his friends.

Jesus was always inviting people to the party or being invited to someone's home for dinner. Sometimes he just invited himself, as when he met Zacchaeus. There was a procession of folks moving through the town, people were crowding around to see and talk with Jesus. Zacchaeus ran ahead of the crowd and climbed a tree to be able to see Jesus as he walked by. I love the story. Jesus stopped the procession and gave Zacchaeus his undivided attention. He was fully present and proximate with Zacchaeus; and then Jesus surprised Zack with an unbelievable invitation: "Come on down from there, let's go to your house for dinner."[19] During the dinner party, Zacchaeus became so excited by the thought of following Jesus that he decided to give away half of his possessions to bless the poor and pay reparation to those he had stolen from. The descending way of Jesus convicted Zacchaeus to the core of his being and gave him new meaning and purpose for life. Prior to the dinner party, Zacchaeus made a living exploiting and deceiving the poor. He valued upward mobility and chased after the accumulation of wealth. His enormous bank account, built on the value of greed and deception, paled in comparison to the love and passion for life that he felt in the presence of Jesus.

What about the meal Jesus shared with Mary and Martha?[20] We don't know how that dinner party turned out, but I like to speculate when reading Scripture. I think the dinner party wound up being a simple meal, maybe just Mary, Jesus, and Martha sharing a sandwich in the living room. At first it's only Mary setting with Jesus, listening to his stories while Martha works frantically in the kitchen. I bet Martha had some big plans with an impressive menu: for starters, they would have her favorite matzo ball soup, followed by her mother's Mediterranean salad, and then a kosher casserole. She has been preparing the menu in her mind for weeks. She wants everything to be perfect and well presented. As Martha swelters and labors over the stove, she finally gets frustrated at her sister for not pitching in and complains to Jesus. "Lord, don't you care that my sister has left me to do the work by myself? Tell her to help me!" I love the way Jesus responds: "Martha, Martha, you are worried and upset about many things, but few things

19. Luke 19:1–9.
20. Luke 10:38–41.

29

are needed—or indeed only one." Most people assume the "one thing" Jesus spoke of was the thing Mary chose—to sit still at the feet of Jesus and listen. That's probably right, but sometimes I wonder. Maybe when Jesus said only one thing is needed, he was saying to Martha: "You're fretting over a big meal—seriously, a sandwich will do. Come on in here and join us."

Big meals are incredible. They create great memories. But sometimes life doesn't get any better than when you share a simple sandwich with a friend over a delightful conversation. Jesus does it all the time. He takes advantage of every meal to be fully present with people, listening to their stories and sharing the story of God's kingdom with them.

The list of dinner parties with Jesus goes on and on. There's the big picnic in the park where everybody in the neighborhood meets up for fish sandwiches, the last supper on the night Jesus is arrested, and the first breakfast on the beach after he comes back to life. One dinner party I enjoy thinking about is the meal he shares with Simon the leper and the "wayward" woman.[21] This scene is a marvelous example of incarnational living and downward mobility. It highlights the importance of living in proximity to the poor.

Get your head around this: Jesus, the Lord of the universe, sets aside his power and his privilege and leaves heaven behind to have lunch with a leper! Rather than going to Simon's house alone, he brings his leadership team to the dinner party. This is a wonderful picture of mission, discipleship, and evangelism all wrapped up together in one expression of incarnational living.

Jesus has a way of taking ordinary experiences—like having lunch with a leper—and turning them into profound teaching moments. I'm sure all the guys around the table were having a great time, sharing lunch with Jesus, talking about religion and politics, maybe one-upping each other with their latest fishing stories. But when the wayward woman crashed the party and started to cry, the mood in the room shifted dramatically. When she started pouring out the expensive perfume on Jesus, these tough guys didn't know what to do or say. As the aroma of her perfume filled the air, somebody broke the silence and said what was on everyone's mind. "This is such a waste! This perfume could have been sold and the money given to the poor!" All the guys nodded in agreement and then turned to Jesus. His reaction was not what they expected. Jesus defended the woman and told them to leave her alone. He quoted some Scripture and pointed out

21. Mark 14:3–9.

the obvious: "The poor you will always have with you." I wonder if he made a gentle hand gesture around the table, or maybe he just put his hand on Simon the leper's hand. Maybe the hand gesture wasn't necessary; his words were profound enough when spoken in the company of the poor who were sitting around the table.[22]

The Scripture Jesus quotes is from Deuteronomy 15:11. It's a passage that expresses God's concern for the poor. It makes the point that the systems of the empire will always make poor people; hence, there will always be poor people living among the people of God. The instruction is clear: God's people are not to be hardhearted or tightfisted; on the contrary, they are to be openhanded toward the poor and needy living in their community. The unspoken message is even more clear; Jesus is saying in bold relief without using words, "You guys have been with me long enough to know I will always be close to the poor. I will always give my time and share my life with them. That's what I do. If you are going to follow me, you will find yourself in proximity with the poor. Therefore, you will always have the opportunity to open your hands and your hearts to share your life and your resources with them."

All of these stories are incredible expressions of God's love for people, but none would have taken place if Jesus had not valued downward mobility. Jesus descended from heaven to live life on life's terms with people. He listened to the stories people told and they longed to hear his. Jesus and his friends built community together and invited the poor from the neighborhood into their lives and shared meals with them. Sharing community at this intimate level was possible because Jesus decided to leave heaven and live in proximity to those who were in great need of good news. These simple, organic experiences of sharing life, sharing meals, and sharing stories were pregnant with opportunities for Jesus to honor his neighbors, build deeper friendships, proclaim good news, reveal God's character, and express the mercy of heaven—which is the goal of downward mobility and incarnational living.

The Table Café

Sometimes when I think about the descending way of Jesus and the simple way he was with people—taking note of how he went about doing good, teaching and healing people in humble and meek ways, sharing meals with

22. Claiborne, *Irresistible Revolution*, 157–61.

friends in the flow of everyday life, creating community, and meeting new friends around the dinner table—I find it hard to believe how complicated we've made it to be and do church. If the church is indeed the body of Christ, it seems to me that life in the church should look something like the way Jesus did life. Let me explain.

When a small group of friends set out to officially plant the Church of the Promise in Portland, rather than focus the majority of our resources on the Sunday morning gathering we looked for a natural way to intersect with our neighbors, Monday through Saturday. The church was meeting for worship in the abandoned warehouse we purchased years before. We renovated some of the space and wanted to discover a relatable way to use the facility to help build community and support economic development in the neighborhood. The metaphor we used to create vision for the space was a "living room." We wanted the warehouse to be a living room for the neighborhood, a third place for people to gather when not at home or work.[23] The house metaphor was on target; we just had the wrong room. Rather than a living room for the community our warehouse became the community dining room, a lunch spot where everybody has a seat at the table.

The Table Café has become a way for us to be present and share proximity with our neighbors as we try to live out the good news. A community café is a relatable space; everybody likes to eat. Let me rephrase that. Everybody *has* to eat. Most people enjoy going out to eat, to share good food with good friends in a pleasant atmosphere. Eating is a common need experienced by everyone regardless of philosophical, political, or theological ideology. Everybody has to eat regardless of his or her economic status. Injustice occurs when some eat and others don't because of economics; or some eat healthy food and others are forced to choose cheap calories—or what most of us call junk food—because it's the only food option available or affordable.

We spent several months listening to our neighbors, trying to discern the felt needs in our neighborhood. What we heard our neighbors express, in multiple ways, was a concern over food insecurity. "We need a place

23. In community-building, the third place is a social surrounding separate from the two predominate social environments of home and the workplace (first and second places). Examples of third places would be environments such as cafés, clubs, restaurants, or civic centers. Historically, the church has been a common third-place gathering for families when not at work or home. We were aware that Portland had few if any third places for our neighbors to gather.

where we can buy some real food!" "We need access to good food we can afford!" "We want a sit-down restaurant!"

First John carries in his heart a huge burden for people living with food insecurity. As we listened to our neighbors he would say, "When people go to bed hungry, they don't feel loved. If we want to love our neighbors, we need to create a meaningful way for hungry people to get something to eat." We knew another food pantry wasn't the right solution. In our search for the next right answer we discovered the pay-what-you-can model for community cafés. It sounded like a good fit for our church and our neighborhood. First John led the way; with a team of friends from our small faith community we created The Table Café. I remember asking First John before we opened the café, "Do you know anything about the restaurant business?" To which he responded, "I've eaten at some good ones." Since none of us knew anything about food service, we established four guiding principles to help us find our way in this uncharted territory.

- *We didn't want to be a church with a restaurant; instead we wanted to have a restaurant where church happens.*[24] Most people are surprised when they discover the café is part of a church, but they notice right away the strange generosity, the radical hospitality, and the fresh expressions of grace offered every day by an odd mix of volunteers.

- *We wanted everyone to have a seat at the table.* No one would be turned away because of social or economic limitations. But we didn't want to be a soup kitchen that serves free meals. We believe you affirm people's dignity at a deep level when you acknowledge everyone has worth and something to give in exchange for goods and services. When you eat at The Table Café you can pay with money or with your time. You can pay the suggested price, a portion of the suggested price, or barter with service. You can even pay it forward by paying more than the suggested price or volunteer your time as a gift so others can have access to good, healthy food at an affordable price.

- *We wanted excellence to be our mode of operation.* When people came to our community café, we wanted them to be surprised by the quality

24. I want to give credit and special thanks to chef Robert Adamson, executive chef and founder of One Bistro in Miamisburg, Ohio, for the mentoring he provided in our initial start-up of The Table Café. One Bistro is a forerunner in the world of pay-as-you-can community cafés. His mentoring, his model, and his experience proved invaluable. The desire to have a restaurant where church happens was a guiding principle of chef Robert's that we adopted for ourselves.

of the food and the service. We wanted to serve local food that was prepared and presented with passion and purpose. We wanted to create an experience our neighbors would not only enjoy but also be proud of.

- *We would not forget we were in the community-building business over and above the restaurant business.* We reinforced this value by printing on the back of our T-shirts, "Enjoy the Flavor of Community." It was our hope that people from the neighborhood, both those with food insecurity and those who just wanted to have lunch at a sit-down restaurant, could enjoy a meal together and build community with their neighbors. We also hoped people from the east side of Ninth Street—an economic and racial divide in our city—would venture over to our side of the street and discover the unique flavor of the Portland community.

At the Church of the Promise we used to have a potluck dinner for church folk once a quarter. Now we have lunch together every day, Monday through Friday, and we invite the whole city to the party. The Table Café is a creative space where people from across the city and all walks of life share proximity and presence. I love it when people from the other side of town dine with us and ask if the "poor people" are coming to the café. Little do they know the family setting next to them, or the hostess who just ushered them to their seat, are the "poor" they're asking about. I will long remember the day when the mayor of our city, a few corporate executives from downtown, some Portland residents, our friends who live under the viaduct, and a lady coming down from an eight-day crack binge experienced proximity as they dined together. As unique as that sounds, it really is just another day in the life of the Church of the Promise at The Table Café.

People who come to volunteer at The Table are given a very brief training—five minutes tops—and a T-shirt. Once they put on the T-shirt they become part of the team, helping to solve the problem of food insecurity in our city. People who were moments before the one in need are now part of the solution. Working side by side, washing dishes, prepping food, and taking time to share a meal helps create an open and trusting atmosphere where we share our life stories with one another. As we listen to the stories of our neighbors and honor them, soon they begin to ask about our story, giving us an opportunity to share the hope that carries us. At The Table, evangelism isn't a weird or forced conversation. We are presented with opportunities daily to offer pastoral care and prayer. We laugh and cry with those who volunteer and share meals with us. We listen and learn from one another. In the mix of it all, the mystery of the gospel is experienced and proclaimed. I have been pleasantly surprised at how organic Christian discipleship flows while chopping carrots with the poor.

Where Are the Poor?

Henri Nouwen was right, the descending way of Jesus will turn our hearts towards the poor; following Jesus' way will lead us in a new direction, down a path of compassion. The challenge for many wealthy Christians is learning how to see the poor who are living among them. The upwardly mobile way of the world has charmed us into building insular communities, some behind gates and walls, where everyone around us looks the same and shares the same level of comfort and economic security. When the words and ways of Jesus interrupt our comfortable lives it awakens a desire to serve the least of these. Those who live in affluent, homogenous neighborhoods are presented with a challenging question and difficult life choices: Where are the poor? And, what cost am I willing to make to share my life with them?

Mother Teresa once said, "You can find Calcutta all over the world, if you have eyes to see. Everywhere, wherever you go, you find people who are unwanted, unloved, uncared for, just rejected by society—completely forgotten, completely left alone."[25] Where is Calcutta in your world? Where are the people who have been rejected, forgotten, and left completely alone? Are they part of your community? Are they included in your church meetings? If not, how might you reorganize your life in order to share presence and proximity with them?

I have a pastor friend named Mike; his church is located in the county seat of an affluent community. He pressed his church to ask this very question. Where are the poor? Mike says, "It's like the trailer park appeared out of nowhere." His church members began to notice—some for the first time—the trailer park on the other side of the town. They knew full well the families from the trailer park were not interested in coming to their church meetings, so they decided to buy a trailer and move in. They deploy interns to live in the trailer with a simple assignment of getting to know and love the neighbors. The women in the church go over to the trailer park every week and read Bible stories to children, and others go over during

25. Glover, "Live Like Mother Teresa," lines 1–4.

the school year to tutor kids. It is a great example of how members from an affluent church can share presence and proximity with people from another community. If the relationships are established with Christlike meekness and humility, they will create the possibility of building authentic friendships and sharing God's love with one another.

Beware: if you choose to make the values of Jesus your very own, you might be inspired to buy a home on the other side of town or move into the trailer park you drove past for years and never noticed. You might start driving home from work another way so you can spend time with a whole new set of friends, who happen to live in a different economic class than you. If you find yourself in that "other place," I want to encourage you to slow down—take the time to listen and learn about life from your new friends. Before you "do" anything, take some cues from Jesus on how to affirm the dignity of other people.

Lord, it was not enough for you to care for the poor. You chose to become one of them by descending as you did. Keep us free from fear and selfish preoccupations that we may walk as you walked among the poor, the sick, and dying in body and spirit. Amen.[26]

---

26. Claiborne et al., *Common Prayer*, 52.

RED LETTER QUESTIONS

Who has touched my clothes?

1. Read Mark 5:21–43. Jesus was close enough to human suffering for a sick woman to touch his clothes, for crowds of people to "press around" him, for a little girl to hold his hand. How does his proximity to human suffering make a difference in the lives of the people discussed in this story?

2. If the value of downward mobility were placed on a continuum from one to ten, with one being the descending way of Jesus, and ten being the upwardly mobile way of the world, where would you place yourself on the scale? If you wanted to embrace the value of downward mobility, how could you move your position on the continuum one step towards the descending way of Jesus?

3. Take a moment and reflect on incarnational living. How are you and your community being present and proximate with the people in your neighborhood? How are you using your power and your influence to love your neighbors and proclaim the gospel in a Christlike way?

4. Where are the poor in your community? How might you share presence and proximity with them?

3

Human Dignity

"We don't move to the margins to serve people; we move to the margins so the margins will cease to exist."

GREGORY BOYLE

"We don't give people dignity, we affirm it."

DR. JOHN PERKINS

"Do to others what you would have them do to you."

JESUS

FOLLOWING THE WAY OF Jesus, making his values our values, will press us to look at ourselves and others and the mission of the church in new ways. We will begin to see the importance of giving balanced attention to the friendship networks that Jesus valued. We will love God with all of our heart, soul, mind and strength. We will truly love our neighbors as we love ourselves—both those on mission with us in the family of God and those neighbors who live far from the center of the church family. We will begin to value downward mobility and seek ways to live an incarnational life in proximity with our neighbors, especially those who live on the margins, those Jesus called the least of these—the poor and the poor in spirit.

Making these simple shifts in our core values might lead us into relationships with people who don't look like us, believe like us, or vote like us. We will be challenged, maybe for the first time, to examine the way we truly feel or think about people from different cultural, ethnic, or economic backgrounds. We may discover the way we treat others, even when we're trying to offer acts of mercy, may offend rather than affirm them as individuals.

Here's an example of what I mean. Before I started thinking about the values of Jesus, I assumed loving the poor meant doing nice things for them. Giving them things. Volunteering time at the soup kitchen or the homeless shelter. Going on church mission trips, better described as "mission-cation" or "volun-tourism." But now I see loving others like Jesus means I will affirm the dignity of every person I meet. Following his way will challenge us to see people as subjects of their own history rather than objects of our charity.[1]

Earlier this summer, Father Greg Boyle spoke at a conference here in Louisville. The conference was called *Love Is Greater than Fear*. Father Boyle is the founder of Homeboy Industries in Los Angeles, a unique ministry that works with gang members from LA. Father Boyle is also the author of a book called *Tattoos on the Heart*.[2]

At the conference, Father Boyle filled the room with amazing stories of grace and followed his stories with provocative questions about love and fear. There was one quote in particular that challenged me to rethink why and how I affirm the dignity of others, especially the poor and those who are pushed to the margins of society. Father Boyle said, "We don't move to the margins to serve people; we move to the margins so the margins will cease to exist."

The image Father Boyle used to define the work of the church was an image of kinship and circles of compassion. The questions he stirred up in my mind are many, but two questions in particular still linger: What would a community look like if we made our circles of kinship so big that everyone was included, where no one was left out? And, how would our cities be impacted if the followers of Jesus really did show compassion and affirmed the dignity of every human being who lived in the city?

Would the so-called margins cease to exist if the people who followed Jesus valued the dignity of others and decided to live in solidarity with

1. Hill et al., *Faith, Religion and Theology,* 396.
2. Boyle, *Tattoos on the Heart.*

marginalized people? Much will have to change to experience the answer. Rather than developing and living in homogenous communities, where everybody looks, acts, and talks in similar ways, we would intentionally design communities and circles of friendship with diversity in mind. Rich and poor, black, white, and every shade in-between, liberal and conservative, gay and straight, would be included in the circle of compassion. This does not mean we must agree with each other's political views or theological beliefs. What it does mean is this: we would make a place at the table for everyone and stay in conversation with each other; we would create protected space, listen to one another, and affirm the God-given dignity of everyone in the circle. If that's the type of space we imagine creating, it would serve us well to observe how Jesus affirmed the dignity of people in his circle.

Jesus Affirms the Dignity of People

Jesus never said, "Verily, verily, I say unto you: affirm the dignity of others," but I'm pretty sure that's what he meant when he told us to "Do to others what you would have them do to you."[3] Likewise, when he was teaching his friends not to look down on others, he told them stories like the parable of a lost sheep to help get his point across. This parable is about a shepherd who owns 100 sheep and has one that wanders away. Jesus says the good shepherd will leave the ninety-nine and go look for the one until he finds it and brings it home. At the end of the parable, Jesus says: "In the same way your Father in heaven is not willing that any of these little ones should be lost."[4] This is a story about human dignity and the value God places on every human soul. Those who were listening to Jesus knew when he finished the story that he valued the dignity of everyone. No one is to be left out! No one is to be left behind! Everyone has equal and inherent value!

It is clear in the teachings of Jesus that one of his core values is affirming the dignity of all people, even the most peculiar of us. However, this value becomes most evident when you consider the way Jesus interacted with individuals and how he honored everyone he encountered. Jesus talks with people who were typically left out of conversations. He hangs out with folks who were isolated from social gatherings. He includes outcasts in his circle of friends. Jesus honors the dignity of others by asking a lot of questions. He is always willing and ready to listen to others and he waits to hear

3. Matt 7:12.
4. Matt 18:14.

what people want or what they need before he steps in and solves their problems. Jesus values the giftedness of others and affirms their dignity by inviting them to share their resources with him.

If our desire is to build a community around the values of Jesus we will seize every opportunity to honor the dignity of others. We can begin by learning from Jesus and imitating the simple ways he affirmed the dignity of those he shared life with.

Jesus affirms the dignity of people who are considered "less-than."

It was no small thing for Jesus to include women and children in conversations. In his context this was far from the norm. Yet, Jesus offers women and children his attention in social spaces and lifts them up as examples when teaching about the kingdom of God. We get a glimpse of this when Jesus has a rather brief but very personal conversation with a Samaritan woman at Jacob's well.[5] In a matter of nineteen verses, they cover subjects like Jewish history and customs, spirituality and the meaning of authentic worship; they talk about theology and truth. And then, Jesus moves the conversation from global and theological issues to a very personal and intimate conversation about the woman's married life. This type of public conversation between a Jewish rabbi and a Samaritan woman would have been unheard of in this woman's world. That's why she's so surprised when Jesus invites her into a conversation by asking her for a cup of water. For Jesus, asking the question and having a public conversation was his way of honoring the dignity of this specific woman on this specific day. It was a simple conversation that changed the woman's life. The inclusion of this conversation in the Gospel of John resounds the message to every woman who reads the story—and every man, for that matter: Jesus values the dignity of women.

He also values and affirms the dignity of children by giving them his time and attention in public settings, another non-traditional position for men to model, especially if you were a Jewish rabbi in the middle of a lecture. Jesus was always drawing a crowd, with plenty of men, women, and children gathering around to hear what he had to say. Some came to hear his stories, others came to be healed; I suppose some came for the fish and bread. In the hustle and bustle of these social gatherings, Jesus created an

5. John 4:7–26.

environment where women felt comfortable and protected. They brought their children to him to receive a blessing from him. The disciples of Jesus thought this was an outrage and rebuked the mothers for disturbing Jesus while he was teaching important things to important people, i.e., the men in the crowd. Jesus took the opportunity to set the disciples straight on the value of children and how to affirm the dignity of people who are left out and pushed to the margins. Jesus takes the children in his arms, places them on his lap, and instantly moves them from the margin to center stage. He blesses the children and lifts them up as an example of kingdom values by saying out loud for all to hear: "Let the little children come to me, and do not hinder them, for the kingdom of God belongs to such as these."[6]

Jesus always has his eye focused on the people who are invisible and passed over by the dominant culture. He sees those who live in the shadows of injustice and shines his light of mercy and grace on them, lifting them out of obscurity by acknowledging their dignity. Jesus is always looking for ways to move people from the margins to the center; or better said, he is always willing to go to the margin to affirm the people who live there.

Jesus affirms the dignity of people by including the excluded in his circle of friends.

Not only are people on the margins affirmed and lifted up as an example to teach others about the social order in the kingdom of God, Jesus includes the excluded in his circle of friends. The Gospel of Luke lets us know there was a group of women with Jesus from the beginning of his ministry. They supported his work out of their own means and they remained with him during his darkest hour.[7] Even though the men abandoned Jesus and went into hiding, the women remained with him at the foot of the cross. The women were there when Jesus was buried, and they were the first to see him after the resurrection. Women were definitely included in his circle of kinship. But there is more to the story.

Page after page in the Gospel narratives we see Jesus including people in his circle of kinship who are typically excluded from social gatherings. He includes sinners. He includes sick and broken people. He includes the poor. He affirms their dignity by sharing life and meals and stories with them. He learns their names. He listens to their concerns. And he touches

6. Luke 18:16.
7. Luke 8:2–3; 23:49.

them. His affirmation of their dignity has a deep healing effect on their lives. Sin is forgiven. Guilt and shame melt away. Demonic strongholds are broken and mental health is restored. Leprosy and paralytic conditions are reversed. There was something profound about the way Jesus affirmed the dignity of people; his affirmation of individuals released a healing presence from heaven into the life of individuals and it affected social structures in redemptive ways.

The value Jesus placed on human dignity helped people see their true identity as children of God. And he helped people recognize and affirm the sacred imprint of God's handiwork in others. His affirmation of human dignity, that includes everyone in an ever-growing circle of compassion, will create a health-releasing, life-giving environment. If this is the kind of community we dream about, we will do well to follow the example of Jesus and make every effort we can to include the excluded.

Jesus affirms the dignity of people by asking questions about their hopes and dreams.

Another way Jesus honors the dignity of others is by listening to their life stories. He invites people to share their stories, as well as their deepest aspirations, by asking questions. The right question, asked in the right way, will create a protected space for people to explore their hopes and dreams.

When Jesus meets Andrew he begins the relationship with a question.[8] At the time, Andrew was a disciple of John the Baptist, hanging out with his teacher on the banks of the Jordan River. Andrew was a seeker of truth, a person looking and waiting to find the Messiah. Perhaps that's why he signed on with John the Baptist. On one particular morning, John points to Jesus and tells his disciples, there goes the Messiah, the "Lamb of God." Andrew and another unnamed man start tagging along behind Jesus, peeking over his shoulder, trying to blend in and not look overly conspicuous. Jesus turns to them and asks a question that invites Andrew into a lifelong adventure. The question is simple, but straightforward: "What do you want?" They spend the rest of the afternoon together. By the end of the day Andrew is convinced that John the Baptist was right. Andrew went and found his brother Simon Peter to tell him they had found the Messiah. The person they had been *longing to meet and hoping to find* was hanging out in the neighborhood.

8. John 1:35–42.

Another place where Jesus asks questions in order to help others explore their hopes and dreams is the conversation he has with two men on the road to Emmaus.[9] It's the third day after the crucifixion and these guys are disheartened. Everything they had lived for over the past three years went up in smoke on the day Jesus was executed. They were leaving the big city and heading for home, to a neighborhood about seven miles away. As they came around a bend in the road Jesus met up with them and began to walk alongside them.

We see a very playful side of Jesus in this story. He intentionally keeps himself from being recognized by his friends and pretends to be someone else. Even when they get to their home in Emmaus, he acts as if he is heading farther down the road. Jesus is quite the thespian in this little drama, waiting to reveal the big surprise at just the right time. What a fun-loving character![10]

Moving undercover, Jesus begins the conversation with a simple question in order to get the men talking. "What are you discussing together as you walk along?" One of the guys, named Cleopas, responds, "Are you the only one in Jerusalem who doesn't know about the things that have happened over the past few days?" And then Jesus asks a second question, "What things?" Sometimes I wonder if Jesus had to work at holding back a self-revealing smile when he asked the second question.

Both men chime in and begin telling the story. They tell this inquisitive stranger on the road all about Jesus. They talk about his prophetic gifts. They reminisce about his powerful teaching and try to explain his extraordinary ability to perform miraculous deeds. They express their frustration and anger at the chief priests and their political leaders, who handed Jesus over to be sentenced to death. As they walk along and share their story, they begin to unpack their grief and unload their heavy hearts with this stranger on the road.

I think it's important to note that Jesus intentionally concealed his identity. He didn't circumvent their grief by revealing the power and glory of his resurrection. Instead he created a safe space for them to process their hope and their despair. The pastoral conversation on the road to Emmaus helped these two men get in touch with the reason for their downcast spirits: "*We had hoped* that he was the one who was going to redeem Israel."[11]

---

9. Luke 24:13–35.

10. Eldredge, *Beautiful Outlaw*, 26–29.

11. Acts 24:21.

44

Later in the evening, when the time was right, Jesus broke bread with them at the dinner table and their eyes were opened. When they realized it was Jesus asking the questions their hope was restored.

Meaningful and sensitive questions, coupled with a listening ear and protected space, will create the opportunity for people to explore their hopes and dreams. When we take our cues from Jesus, we will affirm the dignity of others by asking questions before we answer life's big riddles. Questions, prompted by compassion, will set the stage for the Spirit of God to reveal truth and release hope.

Jesus affirms the dignity of people by asking questions to discern their felt need.

When we pay attention to the conversations Jesus has with people and pay attention to the types of questions he asks, we discover yet another reason why asking questions affirms the dignity of others. Jesus asked questions so he could discern the felt needs of people before he asserted his power to solve their problems. It may sound counterintuitive but when we jump in and start fixing things for people we minimize their pain and devalue their life experience. It is always best to start relationships with questions, especially when we intend to introduce acts of mercy into the friendship.

In Acts 10, we read that "God anointed Jesus of Nazareth with the Holy Spirit and power," and that "he went around doing good and healing all who were under the power of the devil."[12] I absolutely love this image of Jesus, an itinerant preacher who traveled from one town to the next, back and forth across Judea, doing good everywhere he went. At every stop he healed those who were sick and set demonized people free. That sounds like a great way to spend a life.

However, if we want to follow the way of Jesus we need to take note of how he went about doing good. Jesus made it his practice to check with people before meeting their need. Often, before Jesus heals someone, he asks questions and he listens intently to their stories. He discerns their felt need before he heals them. Even when Jesus intuitively knew what they needed, he took the time to build a relationship and to hear their story before he stepped in and asserted his power.

---

12. Acts 10:38.

A good example of where Jesus asked questions before asserting power is when he meets the lame man at the pool of Bethesda.[13] This particular pool was a place where chronically disabled people spent their days. It was a first-century infirmary, a place where the blind, the lame, and the paralyzed would gather in hopes of being healed; or at the very least, having their basic needs met for the day. When the Gospel writer introduces the lame man into the story he describes him as a man who "had been an invalid for thirty-eight years." The word *invalid* literally means non-valid. This man had been "non-valid" for a lifetime. And then Jesus shows up in his life.

Jesus doesn't assume the man wants to be healed; instead he looks into his eyes and asks: "Do you want to get well?" When I read this story, I marvel at the question and wonder to myself: What kind of question is that? How insensitive! Of course the guy wants to get well. Who would choose to live a non-valid life when a life with meaning and purpose is being offered? But then I'm surprised to hear the man's response. Instead of an emphatic *yes*, he gives Jesus a list of excuses, exposing how he has settled into his identity as non-valid. He was comfortable with his role as a dependent person.

Jesus listens to his life story. He listens to the long list of reasons the man gives for the condition of his soul. By asking questions, Jesus honors the man's history and then offers the fellow a new future. For the first time in years, the person talking with Jesus gets in touch with some real hope. After Jesus listens to his story he simply tells the man to, "Get up! Pick up your mat and walk." The healing power of grace and mercy are released in his life and the man walks home, empowered and validated.

We find a similar story in the Gospel of Mark; another example of how Jesus affirms the dignity of others by asking questions and discerning felt needs before asserting his power and influence.[14] Jesus and his band of followers are traveling along the road when they happen to walk by a blind man named Bartimaeus. He is begging for money and hoping for a little social connection. The man knew about Jesus—when you travel from place to place doing good and healing people from the power of the devil the word gets out. When Bartimaeus heard that Jesus of Nazareth was walking by he cried out for mercy: "Jesus, Son of David, have mercy on me!"

Against the protest of others who told the man to be quiet, he shouted out all the more. When Jesus heard the cry, he called for Bartimaeus to

13. John 5:1–15.
14. Mark 10:46–52.

come close. This is the classic mode of operation for Jesus: in the midst of a crowd, while moving through the day with an agenda on his mind, Jesus pauses for interruptions. He gives people in need his undivided attention. He invites them to "come close," to share proximity with him. Jesus, like so many times before, begins the conversation with a question. "What do you want me to do for you?"

Jesus honors his dignity. He doesn't assume to know what the blind man wants. Instead, Jesus creates a space for Bartimaeus to process his faith and reflect on his deepest longing. Bartimaeus uses his own voice to articulate his desire. Jesus then comes along beside him, asserts his power and influence into the relationship and healing follows.

Beloved communities, built around the values of Jesus, will create a protected space where everyone in the community can use their own voice to express their deepest longing and their wildest dreams. Affirming the dignity of others requires that we slow down and listen to their voice in order to discern the felt needs; and then decide together if we have a role in helping them actualize their dreams.

Jesus affirms the dignity of people by inviting them to share their gifts with him.

Another way Jesus affirms the dignity of others is by inviting them to share their resources with him to help meet his needs. That's not something I think about very often, but it's true. Jesus had needs. He was human, and when he got thirsty he needed something to drink. When he got tired he needed a place to rest. When Jesus meets the Samaritan woman at Jacob's well, he is both, thirsty and tired. He sits down by the well for a little rest and engages the woman in a conversation. As we observed in the former section, he begins the conversation with a question, but it is important to note that the question is an invitation for the woman to meet his need. He asks her for a favor, "Will you give me a drink?"[15] Jesus affirms her dignity by acknowledging she had something of worth.[16] She had access to water and he was thirsty.

We see the same pattern when Jesus first meets Simon Peter. Before Jesus invites Peter to follow him, he asks him for a favor. Jesus was teaching on the shore of Lake Gannesaret and he asked Peter if he could use his boat

15. John 4:7.
16. Perkins, *Beyond Charity*, 33–35.

as a platform for teaching. Peter pushes the boat out from the shore, rear-ranges things on the deck, and cleans off a spot for Jesus to sit and teach.[17] There is no doubt in my mind—it was an honor for both Simon Peter and the Samaritan woman to be asked by Jesus to share their resources with him. Asking people to share their gifts and their resources acknowledges they have something of worth to bring to the party of life. Simply asking will affirm their dignity; if they share their gifts it will make for a better party.

Jesus was a man with a mission—a mission to meet needs. He came on a mission to seek and save the lost. He came to give his life as a ransom for many. He set out to preach good news to the poor and set captive people free. He came to serve, not to be served. The irony of the kingdom of God is this: one of the ways Jesus meets our needs and affirms our dignity is by inviting us to join him on his mission and to share our resources with him. He affirms our dignity by suggesting that we have value and worth. He truly believes in us and he invites us to share our gifts with him. We will honor and affirm the dignity of others when we do the same.

Learning to Listen

If building a beloved community around the values of Jesus is our goal, then affirming the dignity of everyone in the community is essential. Point-ing out that Jesus affirmed others by including them in his circle of friends, asking questions, listening to their hopes and dreams, discerning their felt need before asserting his power, inviting them to share their time and re-sources with him, may sound overly simplistic, but it's not so easy to pull off. Listening to others and learning to hear the historical narrative and dreams of a neighborhood takes intentional effort and a lot of time.

If we really desire to listen to the neighborhood, it will take intentional effort to keep ourself and our own agendas out of the way. Even when we know the importance of listening to others, sometimes we forget and fail to listen. Sometimes we get impatient with the process, so we only half listen, or we listen intently for what we want to hear. Any hint of confirmation in favor of our big idea will give us the green light to move full-steam ahead, thinking we have the blessing of others in the community. Genuine listen-ing takes intentional effort.

17. Luke 5:1–3.

Another reason listening requires intentionality is the simple fact that trust is the bottom line for honest and vulnerable conversations, and trust takes time to build. People will give opinions on surveys all day long. They will read, like or unlike, and post comments on Facebook, with or without information, as they drive down the road. No relationship is needed. The people living next door may let you know what they like and don't like about the neighborhood, their neighbors, or even you. But to get real and honest with another person, especially if the person is from another culture, will take time.

If we intentionally place frames around our agendas, and patiently allow for the time required to build credible, trusting relationships, we will begin to hear the deeper desires of our neighbors and the neighborhood. We will begin to hear historical narratives and collective memories. Over time the conversations we have and the relationships we build with our neighbors will be seasoned with laughter and tears, as well as painful memories and hope-filled aspirations. If we're patient and trustworthy, eventually we will be invited into imagining the future with our neighbors, who have been dreaming about the well-being of the neighborhood for generations.

What We Heard

Let me share a couple examples of when we listened well and how listening to our neighbors made all the difference. The Promise Community has been sharing love in Portland since the fall of 1956. That's when Richard and Mary Catherine Slyder showed up on Baird Street. They had one driving passion: to tell children the stories of Jesus. With nothing more than a Bible, an accordion, and a flannel board, they invited every child they could find to join them for what they called a Sidewalk Sunday School. When the fall air turned cold and the amber-colored leaves littered the sidewalk, rather than adorning trees, the children followed the little flannel-board Jesus indoors. The Sidewalk Sunday School became the Sunshine Club and the clubhouse was named the Baird Street Mission. Over the next four decades this Christian ministry specialized in sharing the love of Jesus with children. In 1990, the mission was renamed the Portland United Methodist Center and the leaders of the organization began to wonder what a more holistic model of Christian community development might look like.

We intuitively knew children and youth ministry was imperative; leadership development was a crucial need for our neighborhood. But we began to realize the challenges our neighborhood faced called for a broader, more holistic solution. Spiritual development, though central to our mission, was not enough in isolation from other development initiatives. Education, food insecurity, mental, physical, and emotional healthcare, economic development and job creation, access to decent and affordable housing, and race relations were critical issues that confronted our neighborhood.

Complex layers of social injustice, segregation, and years of economic disinvestment were woven into the historical narrative of the Portland community. Hence, a multifaceted approach to the church's witness in the neighborhood was needed. We started asking: What else could be done? How might we expand the scope of our work and embrace a more holistic approach to our mission? That's when we began asking the values question. How would our approach to ministry change if we really made the values of Jesus our number-one organizing principle? What would we do differently?

Affirming the dignity of our neighbors and listening to them as Jesus did was a value we placed before us. Over the years we have honored that value . . . *most of the time.* However, there have been projects and seasons where the leadership of the Promise Community pushed ahead with some new vision or grand idea without doing a very good job of listening to our neighbors. In hindsight, the projects where our neighbor's voice and their gifts were included made a more lasting impact for positive change than the big ideas that were pursued without our neighbors' input. Planting the church and our recovery program are two ministries in particular where we followed the lead of our neighbors.

Church of the Promise

We never intended to plant a church. It was the voice of our neighbors that prompted us to call the meeting. When parents came to the Center to pick up their children they began asking, "Do you have a worship service on Sunday morning?" If only one or two parents had asked the question I would have thought nothing about it. If only six parents had asked the question, I would have pretended like I didn't hear them. But the neighbors kept asking. Every time we turned around another person would inquire about our worship service, which didn't exist. It made us wonder, was God trying to get our attention?

The neighbors' questions made us curious. Was there a need or a desire for a new faith community in our context? Was this non-profit mission that loved on children after school being asked to create a space for the community to gather and worship? Another telling sign was the simple fact that all the neighbors and the children who came to the center called it "The Church." Everyone who worked there and our volunteers referred to the place as the Center. After all, that's what it said on the sign: Portland United Methodist Center. But it was more than a community center for the families in the neighborhood. It was their church. And, they assumed there would be a place and a time set apart for worship.

When we decided to meet for a season of listening prayer we were clear and well defined: We were not planting a church! We were praying and listening . . . period! There would be no announcements sent out. No brochures. No marketing. No attempt to gather a mass of people for a launch service. The term *attractional church* was not in our vocabulary. If anything we were "unattractional." If someone asked about a worship service, we offered an invitation, otherwise no one knew. This was not the model for church planting that people write books about, but it seemed right for us. It was a covert operation of prayer. Seeking God's heart, listening for God's voice. By the end of the year, I was quite surprised. A small band of neighbors had joined the prayer movement and they were excited to talk about the future of *"our church."*

Celebrate Recovery

After a year of prayerful listening and seeking God's heart there was no turning back. We were a church. Over the course of the year God gave us a vision, a mission, and a promise. The promise was grounded in 2 Chronicles 7:14: "If my people, who are called by my name, will humble themselves and pray and seek my face and turn from their sin, then I will hear from heaven, and I will forgive their sin and will heal their land." Our neighborhood was going to be a "healed land" and the people of God meeting in the chapel of our obscure, non-profit community center would play a vital role in the healing process.

There was one thing most of the folks who showed up for prayer on Sunday morning shared in common: we all had personal experience with compulsive or addictive behaviors. Most of us knew, far too well, the emotional and spiritual hurt brought on a family by drug and alcohol abuse.

We were well-versed in unhealthy habits, and collectively we had a long list of pathological hang-ups. As we listened to one another and sought God's heart it seemed obvious that the crosshairs of our church's mission would be focused on people who needed help recovering from life's hurts, habits, and hang-ups. At the beginning of our second year we launched a Celebrate Recovery program and set out to be a church for and with people in recovery. After nineteen years of growing into our vision, I still tease our community of faith and tell people that half of our church is in recovery . . . and the other half needs to be.

I'll never forget the day when Joe showed up at the prayer meeting. It was early on, back when six people would have been considered a crowd. No one else had arrived. I was alone and praying in the corner of the room. When I stood up and turned around Joe was standing in the doorway. As we made eye contact he said, "Pastor Larry, I need to be saved!" Not, "Hello." Not, "Can we sit and talk?" Not, "How are you today?" His first word was a prayer for help. "I need to be saved!"

"Being saved" is a loaded phrase and means different things to different people. To my friend Joe it meant he was losing his family, his career, his home, and his future because of a gambling addiction. He didn't know where else to turn, so he turned to Jesus. Joe and his family joined the prayer movement for a season and provided valuable leadership when we decided to offer a Celebrate Recovery program for the community. Joe discovered new levels of hope and freedom through his friendship with Jesus. He rebuilt his life and he built a new home for his family. No doubt about it, Joe's family is a shining star in our neighborhood.

Paul and Mary Jolly joined the prayer movement shortly after Joe's family. The Jollys were somewhere on a continuum between agnostic and atheist. They weren't looking to answer the "God question," nor did they have "Being a part of a church family" on their bucket list. However, on Father's Day they came to visit our prayer group to appease Paul's dad. They were both surprised by the love and the community they discovered, and equally surprised by their desire to keep coming back. Both Paul and Mary are adult children of alcoholics. They were deeply aware of the negative effect codependency has on interpersonal and family dynamics. Father's Day was the beginning of a spiritual journey for Paul and Mary that would eventually lead to freedom from their unhealthy life-script. It was a grand celebration on the day we baptized them into the family of God. The church was there for Joe, and for Paul and Mary, because we listened to our neighbors.

On the day Mary was baptized she invited her friend Rhonda to the celebration. Rhonda had visited our Celebrate Recovery meeting a few times but had not darkened the door of a church meeting in years. She had a long history of drug abuse that left a wake of emotional wreckage. When Rhonda showed up at our Celebrate Recovery meeting she had been sober for a while but serenity was a foreign concept. She tells people now that she got the sober part but missed the spiritual part. To her, God was more of a higher recluse than a higher power. During Mary's baptism, the Holy Spirit surprised Rhonda with the awareness that God loved her too and there wasn't anything she could do about it. Not long after Mary's baptism, the church family circled around Rhonda and celebrated with her as she too was baptized into the family of God.

Mary and Rhonda are best friends. They have worked side by side, leading our Celebrate Recovery program for years. Every Thursday night fifty to seventy-five men and women come to the Promise Building to share a meal, hear a message of hope, and build healthy relationships that will encourage them on their road to recovery. More important than being best friends, Mary and Rhonda are sisters in Christ. They are neighbors who love each other and they spend countless hours scheming new ways to express God's love in our neighborhood.

Affirming people, listening to their hopes and dreams, and supporting the lead of neighbors like Mary and Rhonda have made a positive and lasting impact in our neighborhood. Our neighbors are leading the way as we pursue God's promise together and enjoy the wonder of God's life-affirming, healing presence.

I can imagine a world without margins, a place where no one is left out.
If we follow Jesus to the margins of society and share life with people who
are forced to live there—treating our neighbors the way we want to treated,
creating circles of kinship that include and affirm the dignity of everyone—
the so-called margins will cease to exist.

RED LETTER QUESTIONS
Do you see this woman?

1. Read Luke 7:36–50. In this story we meet a woman who "lived a sinful life." She interrupts a dinner party hosted by a Pharisee named Simon. The woman pours expensive perfume on the feet of Jesus and wipes his feet with her hair. Simon is offended by the woman's presence and the way Jesus affirms her. Jesus looks at Simon and asks him a direct question: "Simon . . . Do you see this woman?" The Bible doesn't say how or if Simon answered the question. How do you think he responded? Did Simon see a woman with inherent dignity, in need of affirmation, or did he see a "prostitute" to be shunned?

2. The Scripture doesn't say the woman was a prostitute. It simply says she was a "sinner." Traditionally, when people have preached or written about this woman she has been identified as a prostitute. Discuss possible reasons why tradition has ascribed the sin of this woman as a sexual sin? Can you imagine other scenarios why her life was a wreck? Regardless of her past or her reputation, Jesus saw a child of God, a sister with inherent dignity that needed to be affirmed. How did he affirm her dignity?

3. Who in your context is invisible to the public eye? Since they are invisible it may take some intentional work to answer this question. Spend time this week trying to see and discern who is being overlooked, ignored, or shunned by you or your community; and then discuss ways you and your community can affirm their dignity.

4. Below are four exercises to help you listen to your neighbors. Pick one or two and practice the spiritual discipline of listening.

   • Set apart a season for prayer walking in your neighborhood. Meet on a specific day of the week, for four to eight weeks. Deploy small groups of people to walk in different directions. Observe and listen as you walk. Meet back together and share observations. Pray together and be sure to pay attention to what the Holy Spirit might be showing you about your neighborhood.

- Make a list of community events and gatherings that your neighbors deem important. Plan to attend those events. Listen and learn. Report back to the group what you heard.

- Identify a few elders in your neighborhood. Invite yourself to their front porch for a cup of coffee and conversation. Listen to their stories and their memories. Listen to their dreams.

- Make a list of other ways you can listen to your neighbors and put one of them into practice.

4

Radical Generosity

"God is always trying to give good things to us,
but our hands are too full to receive them."

AUGUSTINE

"You're far happier giving than getting."

JESUS

DO YOU EVER WONDER why some people are more generous than others? Some people will give you the shirt right off their back, while others barely give you the time of day. I know we're supposed to love everybody; but truth be told, I like generous people more than stingy people. Generous people make me smile. They add life to a community and they appear to be happier than those who are tight-fisted and obsessed with hoarding everything they can.

When I think about the disparity between the generous people I know and their stingy counterparts, it becomes apparent to me that generosity exists on a continuum. I live with a person who falls on the generous end of the scale, while I fall on the more reserved side. I know this about myself because my generous wife, who likes to volunteer and help others, says when I'm asked to do something for somebody my first response is always, "No." Even when I change my mind after saying no, or catch myself before I say no and agree to give a little of my time, Kathie says my body language betrays my yes. She sees and feels the invisible boundary I put up, even when others don't.

I want to be more generous. I want to be the person who gives freely and adds life to the party. When I leave a party, I want others to be glad I showed up, instead of being glad I'm gone. I want my life to be infectious, causing others to be happy and inspired to be more generous themselves. That's exactly how generous people make me feel—happy and longing to be more generous.

I think Jesus was that kind of person. He gave everything he had to make God's extravagant love known to people. Jesus valued generosity. He gave all of his possessions. He gave his time. He gave his power. He even gave his life. He was, in more ways than one, the life of the party! People were glad to be in his presence.

Well, almost everyone! There were some who were threatened by his radical generosity and jealous of his popularity. They were the tight-fisted, stingy people who hoarded privilege, power, and social position for themselves. When they were confronted with the radical generosity of Jesus, they were afraid they might lose some of their own power, so they decided to kill him.[1] Radical generosity has the ability to bring out the best in us, or the worst. Either we become more free and self-giving, or we shrink back and believe the lie that there's not enough to go around, holding on tighter to the little we do have.

The virtue of generosity is best understood when placed on a continuum. On the one end is an altruistic lifestyle that believes in the superabundance of God's resources and freely gives good things to others. On the other end of the continuum is a consuming lifestyle that hoards resources with an insatiable desire for more. If we are serious about following the way of Jesus and have any hope of building a community based on his values, we will make an honest assessment of where we fall on the continuum and then make a conscious decision to lead the community toward a more benevolent life.

Created in the Image of a Generous God

I love reading the creation stories in the Bible. They help me hold out hope for the world we live in. It is good for my soul to be reminded that we humans are created in the image of God. I know we don't act like it most of

1. John 11:45–53.

the time, but it's true. A self-giving, loving, and radically generous God created us in God's image and placed us in a garden full of resources that God called "good." We were commissioned to take care of the place, to steward the good and abundant resources, and to care for all of the other inhabitants that lived there.

Our story begins in paradise, but it doesn't turn out so well. By the end of Genesis chapter four the place is a wreck. Everything was going fine until a serpent entered the story and deceived Adam and Eve, tempting them to eat the forbidden fruit. More is lost than Adam and Eve's innocence; God has to sacrifice an animal and make some clothes to cover their bare-butt shame. Their two sons can't get along. Cain gets overrun with jealously. He's convinced his brother Abel possesses something of more value than what he has. Sibling rivalry and competition consume Cain's heart, and he reacts violently toward his brother.

Paradise unraveled when the snake whispered into the ear of those first humans and suggested there wasn't enough in the garden to meet all of their needs. There was that one thing that was prohibited. *Surely life would be better if you went after the one thing God told you not to consume.*

The snake's lie got the best of Cain as well. *If you can't have more than your brother, or if your brother possesses something of more value than what you have, the best solution is to subdue, conquer, and eliminate the competition.* The worthless snake messed up everything. His myth of scarcity[2] wrecked the garden and has deceived every generation since.

The rest of the Bible reads like God's reconstruction project. From Genesis chapter five to the end of the book, God works to clean up the mess. God organizes a group of people and sends them out to remind everyone and demonstrate to the world that we are indeed created in God's image, and the world we live in is designed to look like heaven—a paradise filled with good and abundant resources to be shared and enjoyed by everyone.

Jesus Reveals a Generous God

After several attempts at reconstruction—organizing and reorganizing the people of God, sending leaders like Moses to liberate, anointing kings like David to protect, and calling on prophets like Elijah to correct—God sends the Son of God to put the world back on a trajectory towards paradise. In the life of Jesus, we receive a flesh-and-blood example of what living a fully

2. Brueggemann, "Liturgy of Abundance."

human life that reflects the image of God is like. In the Gospel of John, Jesus makes it clear to his closest friends that he has come to reveal the nature of God: "If you have seen me, you have seen my Father."[3]

When I look at Jesus, I see extravagant, self-giving love. The apostle John saw the same thing. After spending three years with Jesus he concluded, "God so loved the world that *he gave* his one and only son . . . to save the world through him."[4]

God's radical generosity is a constant theme in the stories Jesus tells.[5] I love it when Jesus uses humor in his stories to help emphasize his point. Surely people chuckled when he told the one about the dad who considered giving his children a snake and a scorpion for supper instead of bread and fish! After the laughter stopped, Jesus delivered the punch line: "If you then, though you are evil, know how to give good gifts to your children, how much more will your Father in heaven give the Holy Spirit to those who ask him!"[6]

In addition to the stories he told, we realize the value Jesus placed on generosity by the way he celebrated and encouraged people who acted generously. Consider his reaction to the poor widow who gave all she had as an offering to God. Jesus lifts her gift up as an example of extreme generosity by saying, "This poor widow has put in more than all the others. All these people gave their gifts out of their wealth; but she out of her poverty put in all she had to live on."[7] Or, consider the way Jesus responded when Zacchaeus vowed to give half of his possessions to the poor and pay reparations to those he had stolen from. "Today salvation has come to this house!"[8]

These words and ways of Jesus lift up the generous nature of God. But Jesus didn't just talk about God's excessive generosity; he demonstrated it in the way he lived and shared his life with people. Saint Paul summarizes the generous way of Jesus by saying, "Even though he was rich, yet for [our] sake he became poor, so that [we] through his poverty might become rich."[9] Jesus set aside his position and the glory of heaven, he gave up his job in the wood-shop and left his home in Nazareth, he gave everything he had—his time, his money, his energy, his life—to make God's generous love known

3. John 15:24.

4. John 3:16–17.

5. Matt 6:19–21; 10:40–42; Luke 6:38; 10:25–37.

6. Luke 11:13.

7. Luke 21:3–4.

8. Luke 19:9.

9. 2 Cor 8:9.

on Earth. This is why we experience God's love at a deep and personal level when we look upon the cross of Christ and realize Jesus laid down his life for the salvation of the world.

It is essential to recognize that Jesus *gave his life* as a way to break the curse of sin and death; his life was not taken from him by a power greater than his love for God and people. Jesus *gave his life* as an expression of love and allowed the principalities of this world to crucify him. His self-giving love exposed the brutality of injustice and the limits of sin and evil. The darkness of this world did its worst when it crucified the Son of God. Evil extended its reach to its utmost limit. Evil did all it could do, but it did not have the final word. God's extravagant, self-giving love had the capacity to reach far beyond the limits of sin and evil. God's love is eternal and abundant. It will never quit doing good! It will never run out! There is no scarcity in God's love!

Whenever the weight of evil presents itself and wreaks havoc on this good world, it is right for the people of God to stand firm and proclaim again the story of God's extravagant love expressed in the life, death, and resurrection of Jesus. By the power of the risen Christ, we will do even more than proclaim the story; we will live it! Beloved communities that desire to align their values with the values of Jesus will comprehend the "great love [God] has lavished on us, that we should be called children of God."[10] As children created in God's image, we can chase after a generosity that looks like Jesus.

Chasing After a Generous God

Whenever I compare the radical, self-giving life of Jesus to my personal practice of giving, it drives me nuts. I have a long way to go in order to live out the generous way of Jesus. I have much to unlearn about the consumerist ways of this world that are based on the myth of scarcity, and even more to learn about the economics of God's super-abundant kingdom. An honest assessment of Christian congregations in North America would reveal the same to be true in the majority of our local churches. Christian congregations in our Western context fall far short of exemplifying Christlike generosity.[11]

10. 1 John 3:1.
11. Schultz, "Shocking Truth," lines 16–23.

60

However, the disparity between the two must not prevent us from chasing after the radical generosity of Jesus. We can practice generosity as a spiritual discipline, and in so doing, we can learn new levels of freedom, joy, and creativity. We can reclaim God's narrative for us and begin to live out God's original design for community—a benevolent and beloved community created in the image of God that shares the good gifts of God freely and abundantly with one another.

From time to time throughout church history, we see glimpses of individuals or communities of faith pressing into Christlike generosity. In the Acts of the Apostles, we read about the People of the Way, those early followers of Jesus who chased after God's vision of a beloved community. They understood kingdom economics and believed in the super-abundant resources of God. They were generous and enjoyed giving their possessions to meet the needs of the poor who lived among them.

> All the believers were one in heart and mind. No one claimed that any of their possessions was their own, but they shared everything they had. With great power the apostles continued to testify to the resurrection of the Lord Jesus. And God's grace was so powerfully at work in them all that there were no needy persons among them. For from time to time those who owned land or houses sold them, brought the money from the sales and put it at the apostles' feet, and it was distributed to anyone who had need.[12]

Those first followers of Jesus got it. Some of them rubbed elbows with Jesus for three years and watched as he gave all he had for the well-being of others. His self-giving love inspired them to chase after his way of generosity.

Seventeen hundred years later, a preacher named John Wesley got it. The founder of the Methodist movement left an example worthy of chasing. He wrote down a ton of instructions for any who wanted to follow his "method" of living out one's faith in Jesus. Some of those instructions spoke directly to the management of one's time and resources. There is a saying, widely ascribed to Wesley that summarizes his view on stewardship:

Do all the good you can,
By all the means you can,
In all the ways you can,
In all the places you can,
At all the times you can,

12. Acts 4:32–35.

To all the people you can,
As long as ever you can.

John Wesley did more than write about radical generosity—he lived it. This is the man who said, "If I leave behind me ten pounds . . . you and all mankind bear witness against me, that I lived and died a thief and a robber."[13] Wesley believed the abundant life Jesus promised was found in more of God, rather than in more of this world's wealth, so he practiced a simple axiom of stewardship: "Earn all you can; save all you can; give all you can."[14] A survey of his income and giving patterns, done by Charles White, reveals the extent to which he governed his financial affairs by this: *earn all, save all, give all* principle:

> In 1731 Wesley began to limit his expenses so that he would have more money to give to the poor. He records that one year his income was 30 pounds and his living expenses 28 pounds, so he had 2 pounds to give away. The next year his income doubled, but he still managed to live on 28 pounds, so he had 32 pounds to give to the poor. In the third year, his income jumped to 90 pounds. Instead of letting his expenses rise with his income, he kept them to 28 pounds and gave away 62 pounds. In the fourth year, he received 120 pounds. As before, his expenses were 28 pounds, so his giving rose to 92 pounds.[15]

Wesley's radical generosity perplexes my mind and stretches my imagination. But I'm not the only one perplexed by his radical generosity. He also baffled the minds of his peers, especially the English tax commissioners. In 1776, they inspected his return and sent a letter stating: "[We] cannot doubt but you have plate for which you have hitherto neglected to make an entry."[16] I wonder what they did with the letter Wesley sent in response: "I have two silver spoons at London and two at Bristol. This is all the plate I have at present, and I shall not buy any more while so many round me want bread."[17] Wesley's heart was pricked deeply by the pain of those who suffered under the relentless burden of poverty. He was convinced the appropriate

13. Wesley, *Works of the Rev. John Wesley*, 215.
14. Harnish, *Simple Rules for Money*, 5.
15. White, "What Wesley Practiced," lines 26–33.
16. White, "What Wesley Practiced," lines 44–45.
17. White, "What Wesley Practiced," lines 47–49.

response for the follower of Jesus was threefold. First, apply one's self in gainful employment, earning as much as you can. Second, save a surplus by managing your financial resources wisely and thriftily, spending as little as you possibly can to supply for your personal need. Third, give the remainder of your resources away, to relieve the pain of the poor.

When John Wesley died in 1791, at the age of eighty-seven, the only money mentioned in his will was the miscellaneous coins found in his pockets and dresser drawers. White's survey suggests that during his lifetime, Wesley earned around 30,000 pounds, which in today's currency would be approximately thirty million dollars. I don't know about you, but Wesley's model of radical generosity makes me pause. It challenges me to reflect on my own patterns of getting and giving. The bottom line is this; he makes me want to be more generous.

People like John Wesley and the early church in Acts serve as prophetic examples of radical generosity. Contemporary communities of faith that want to look like Jesus will be inspired by historic examples of kingdom economics and will make the decision to chase after Christlike generosity.

There Is Always More

The choice we made to chase after Christlike generosity taught our community several truths about kingdom economics. First and foremost, we discovered in God's super-abundant kingdom there is always more! There is more to give, more to receive, and more to learn. In addition to learning that God will supply adequate resources to fulfill God's mission, we discovered four other life-giving lessons.

Generosity Is Fun

Church of the Promise is not a wealthy church by any stretch of the imagination. We are small in number, and the majority of our church family lives below the poverty line. When we first began meeting on Sunday morning for a time of prayer, we put a basket in the back and invited people to put money in the basket on their way out of the chapel . . . if they wanted to. On some occasions, our neighbors with great financial need would take money out, rather than put money in. The rationale behind our low-key method of receiving an offering was a desire to not embarrass anyone who came to the meeting with empty pockets.

At that time in our history, the good will of benevolent donors, who lived on the other side of town, supported the operational budget of the Promise Center. When we decided to make our community of faith an "official" congregation of the United Methodist Church, our leaders said they wanted to help pay for the expenses of the church. No longer would the offering basket be hidden in the back of the room; we would pass it around the circle during worship. The newly appointed finance committee said we needed two people to count the offering for accountability's sake. The next Sunday, two of us met in my office. I looked in the basket and said, "It looks like five dollars to me. What do you see?" They agreed. We signed the accounting slip and deposited our first official offering in the bank on Monday morning.

To help reinforce the value of generosity, we decided to give away 20 percent of all the money we received, whether it came from our Sunday morning offering or from our wealthy friends on the other side of town. We called the 20 percent gift a *relational tithe*.[18] Granted, we don't have a very large budget. Twenty percent of "not much" is 80 percent less than "a little bit." But the size of the gift is not the point; the point is cultivating a generous heart in the life of the church.

Our leadership team meets every quarter to do what church committees do. Unlike most churches where I served in the past, the best part of the meeting is the finance report. We have a blast deciding where to give the relational tithe. One of the lessons we learned while chasing after a generous God is that Jesus was right: "You're far happier giving than getting."[19] It is fun to give good gifts freely and abundantly to others. *But there's more.*

Generosity Increases Your Capacity

Another thing we learned about generosity is this: resources given freely and abundantly will increase your capacity to bless others in helpful ways, beyond your personal limits. Our practice of giving the relational tithe is to support other non-profit ministries in the neighborhood that share common values with us and meet the needs of our neighbors in ways we don't have the capacity or skill set to meet. The relational tithe leverages

18. We borrowed this name from Relational Tithe, Inc., an organic, friendship-based, nonprofit that facilitates the giving of resources to support and meet the needs of people. The goal of the nonprofit is to eliminate economic isolation.

19. Acts 20:35 MSG.

20 percent of our income to assist our neighbors in ways we could never dream of doing on our own. The collaborative partnerships we've created offer a more holistic approach to meeting needs. Together, we accomplish far more than we could have ever accomplished if we kept the resources to fund our own programs.[20]

Giving good gifts freely and abundantly is fun. Generosity will leverage other kingdom resources for the common good of a neighborhood. But, *there is still more.* Generosity is contagious.

Generosity Is Contagious

I have a friend who claims his spiritual gift is making money. I'm not sure if making money is a spiritual gift or not. It certainly doesn't show up on Saint Paul's list of gifts in the Bible. But if it is a spiritual gift, this guy received a double portion. When he sold his business, he established a foundation and set out to give away a massive amount of money. He would call me up now and then to talk about his next philanthropic adventure. Somewhere in the conversation he would always say, "Larry, you can't out-give God, but it sure is fun trying!"

My friend has two great passions: worship and prison ministry. He spent every Sunday for a decade going to prison to worship with inmates. He wanted to bless the friends he made in prison but giving them money was considered contraband, so he decided to build his incarcerated friends a new chapel. He did the same thing for a small Methodist college here in Kentucky. He loved the mission of the school and the students he met there. So he built a Christian Ministry Center on the campus. He fell in love with a ministry in Africa, and guess what? He helped the pastors there create spaces for worship and prayer. He did the same for us. As soon as my friend discovered we were building a Christian Community Center in the neighborhood, he surprised us with a jumbo-sized donation. There is no doubt about it: my friend is gifted at making money, but his real spiritual gift is the gift of giving.

I'll never forget the conversation we had when I was telling him about our plans to create a pay-what-you-can community café:

20. Some of our relational ministry partners at the time of this writing include Fed with Faith, Hosea's House, Choose Well, Portland Promise Center, and the Table Café.

Larry, are you really going to let people pay whatever they can afford for a meal?

That's the plan.

And if they don't have any money, you plan to give them a meal anyway, in exchange for some volunteer time?

Yes . . . Do you think we're crazy?

It's not crazy. It's brilliant! This is the best idea I've ever heard! *You're going to lose a lot of money!* But it's a great idea.

Even though others expressed the same concern and warned that people would take advantage of a café operating with a pay-what-you-can policy, we made the decision to roll the dice and place our bet on generosity. What we discovered early on, only months after the café opened, is that generosity is extremely contagious. People enjoy doing good things for other people. When you create an environment based on generosity, the goodwill of one person inspires the goodwill of another.

Our business model required that 70 percent of our customers pay the suggested price of the meal and give a little extra to pay it forward, so the remaining 30 percent could eat for less than the suggested price. For our non-profit café to be sustainable, we needed the average pay-it-forward donation to be at least 25 percent over the suggested price of the meal, and we needed to serve a minimum of eighty meals a day.

We were pleasantly surprised to watch the phenomenon of generosity unfold at The Table Café. Instead of eighty people a day, we serve an average of 125. The pay-it-forward donation is closer to 35 percent, rather than 25. And the number of volunteers eager to be a part of this expression of kingdom economy has been overwhelming. The first year of operation, we had over 900 people from all over the city volunteer time at the café, either to pay for their meal or to help pay it forward for the next person.

The best story of all is the Friday morning when we had a person pay for all of the open tickets in the café. It was a blast telling people when they came to the counter to pay for their meal that someone else had already taken care of it. One by one, they would smile and then say, "Well, let me pay for the next person's meal." All day long, for the remainder of the day, no one paid for his or her own meal. But they did enjoy paying for the next person's. Generosity works that way, it is contagious. I think my friend was right; you can't out-give God, but it sure is fun trying!

A community based on the values of Jesus will take seriously the economy of God's super-abundant kingdom. They will share good things with others, freely and abundantly. The joy they receive from giving will affect the ethos of the community and a contagious culture of generosity will be created. *But there is still more!* The ripple effect that goes out from this generous community will produce immeasurable results.

Generosity Creates Supernatural and Immeasurable Results

The Bible story that best demonstrates the supernatural potential hidden in a simple expression of generosity is the story in which a little boy shares his lunch with Jesus.[21] After Jesus receives the boy's gift of five biscuits and two fish, he blesses it, breaks it, and feeds over 5,000 people—with twelve baskets of leftovers. The number of baskets of leftovers is significant; the story implies there are enough leftovers to feed all twelve tribes of Israel if they want in on the picnic.

I've always wondered, when did the miracle of multiplication happen in this story? Did it happen in the boy's hands? Every time he reached into his lunch box to give Jesus a biscuit, did another one appear? Or did the multiplication happen when Jesus blessed the food and broke it? Maybe it happened in the disciples' hands after Jesus sent them out to distribute the fish sandwiches to the people on the hillside that had been organized into small groups. Or did the multiplication happen in the smaller groups? Sometimes a culture of generosity happens swifter when the larger community is organized in smaller clusters, held together with a common purpose. I have a friend who says the multiplication happened in the hands of the women who were at the picnic but not counted in the 5,000. She is certain that the Jewish women came prepared to feed their children, and when they saw the generosity of the little boy they were inspired to share their resources with all the men who didn't think ahead or bother to bring a lunch basket.

I have no idea when or how the multiplication happened. What I do know is this: God can do a lot with a little when we give God all we've got. A small gift, released into the hands of Jesus, will have immeasurable results.

---

21. Matt 14:13–21; Mark 6:30–34; Luke 9:10–17; John 6:2–15.

If a community buys into the myth of scarcity and spends all of its energy looking at the need rather than looking at their assets, they will respond more like Philip in the story. When Jesus asked him, "Where shall we buy bread for these people to eat?" Philip responded, "It would take more than half a year's wages to buy enough bread for each one to have a bite!"[22] But if the community believes in God's super-abundant kingdom and the power of generosity, they will focus on the assets of the community. Even if their resources are limited, they will respond more like Andrew, who said, "Here is a boy with five small barley loaves and two small fish, but how far will they go among so many?"[23]

The community that believes in God's super-abundant resources will leverage the community's assets for the common good. It will place them in the hands of Jesus. He will receive them, give thanks, and multiply them in miraculous ways. The meager gifts, given in love, will have a miraculous and immeasurable impact on the welfare of the community. God can do a lot with a little if we give God all we've got.

I saw this supernatural phenomenon happen when my friends, Art and Josephine, gave all they had to the church—a gift which would be considered as insignificant in the eyes of most people. But in God's economy it was a great expression of love, big enough to bless a multitude of people.

Art and Josephine were siblings who never married and lived together on Baird Street their entire lives. They lived in a tiny, three-room shotgun house from the day they were born until the day they died. The house sat across the street from the Promise Center. Whenever the hyper-activity of mindless middle-school children got the best of me—which was a weekly experience—I would slip away and visit with Art and Josephine.

The front room of the house doubled as Art's bedroom and the living room for hosting company. They were always glad to see me, and both of them would insist I sit in the overstuffed chair next to Art's bed. Josephine would sit on the end of the bed and Art would sit across the room in a foldable lawn chair. Before my butt hit the chair, Josephine would offer me a cup of coffee. She never waited for an answer; she just shuffled off to the kitchen and moments later, returned with three cups of instant Sanka coffee. With the noise of middle-school kids fading in my mind, I would settle into the chair, sip on the Sanka, and listen to Art and Josephine share a lifetime of memories.

22. John 6:5–7.
23. John 6:9.

I enjoyed listening to their stories of days gone by. Life in Portland. Adventures on Baird Street. How things had changed. How they remained the same. They knew every child who lived on the street by name and told tales on all their parents. Art talked often about his career as an iceman; how he and his brother Pete delivered ice from one end of Portland to the other. Josephine talked about her days working in the department store around the corner and what it was like to clean houses for families on the other side of town. They loved telling stories about their brother Pete, who died long before I met the Barkers. Pete joined the army when he was young and "got out of Baird Street." Their eyes would twinkle with pride whenever they showed me the postcards he sent them from around the world.

As the two grew older and their health began to fail they had no one to care for them. They had no blood relatives. No children. No aunts, uncles, or cousins. All they had to lean on were a handful of friends from Baird Street and the church family next door. The weeks leading up to Art's death were spent in the hospital. I would visit Art once a week and leave the hospital with a special assignment. The first assignment was to go to his kitchen, look in the cupboard behind the flour, and get the money hidden there. Sure enough, tucked behind the bag of flour was a Sanka coffee jar filled with old coins. Several of the coins were from other countries, souvenirs Pete had sent home to his brother and sister.

On the next visit I was instructed to look in the bedroom closet, on the top shelf behind the magazines, get the box and give it to the church. It was like a treasure hunt. I did as I was told and found an old cigar box, covered with a decade of *Life* magazines. In the box was a small fortune: $117.

This gifting of hidden treasures went on for weeks. "Get the title to my car and give it to Junior." "Find my gun under the bed and give it to Bert." "Out in the shed is an old handmade tool box filled with ice tongs. I want you to have the box."

The final gift was the house. Art and Josephine wanted the church to have it. They gave the tiny, three-room house that had been their home for their entire lives to the only family they had.

We received the gift. We gave thanks and blessed it. And then we broke it and gave it away, much like Jesus did with the fish and bread. The house was far too small and too rundown to restore. So we demolished the house, turned half of the property into a park that I fondly call Barker Memorial Park and gave the rest of the property to Habitat for Humanity.

We collaborated with five United Methodist churches in the city and built three Habitat homes on the property. We called the project Miracle on Baird Street. At the house blessing of the third home, we threw a big party. Balloons everywhere. Punch and cookies covered the picnic tables in Barker Park. The streets were lined with people from the other side of town who sponsored the three houses. Volunteers who helped build the houses crowded together on the front lawn. Curious neighbors stood on the sidewalk. Rob Lock, the local director of Habitat for Humanity, stood on the front porch with the new homeowner of the third house, a single mom and her five-year-old daughter. Her eyes filled with tears as Rob handed her the keys to the house. She expressed appreciation to everyone who helped make her dream a reality and then she slowly turned and opened the door to her new home. Applause echoed up and down the street, balloons lifted from the ground and dotted the sky. When the noise settled down, Rob thanked those who made the Miracle on Baird Street possible and then said, "This project has brought our attention to Portland. These are the first three houses we've built in the neighborhood, but they will not be the last. We plan on building a lot more homes here in the years to come."

The Miracle on Baird Street was nineteen years ago. Since then, Habitat for Humanity has built twenty-one homes in a three-block radius around Barker Park and another 105 homes throughout the Portland neighborhood. In 2011, they renovated an abandoned warehouse in the neighborhood and moved their entire operation into Portland. Shortly after they moved in, they opened a Habitat ReStore a few blocks south of Baird Street—a place where neighbors can purchase used furniture and used building supplies at an affordable price.

A multitude of people—and the number is rising—are blessed every day through the work of Habitat for Humanity. People from the neighborhood shop in the ReStore. Volunteers experience the joy of giving their time to help build homes for others. Hundreds of new homeowners and their children experience the security and the joy of owning their own home. All of these blessings are mysteriously connected to one simple act of generosity, a gift given by a poor man and his sister.

Art and Josephine didn't own much, but what they did have, they gave to Jesus. He received the gift, he blessed it, he broke it, and he gave it away. Jesus multiplied the gift, and others, for generations to come will receive benefit from the gift. No one will ever know the source of the original gift that set this multitude of blessings into motion. Generosity is mysterious, it will set in motion a supernatural phenomenon that produces immeasurable results. God can indeed do a lot with a little when we give God all we've got.

A community that chases after the values of Jesus will be known for its radical generosity! Contagious joy will be woven into the social fabric of the community because we are far happier when we give than when we receive. The size of the gift won't matter; small and simple acts of generosity will multiply and remind the world that our story began in a super-abundant garden called paradise.

God, whose giving knows no end, make us glad recipients of your generosity. Give us eyes to see and ears to hear and hearts to remember your abundance, that we might share it with the world. Amen.[24]

24. Brueggemann, *Celebrating Abundance*, 8–9.

Think Red

RED LETTER QUESTIONS

Whose image is this?

In Mark 12:13–17, a group of Pharisees set out to trap Jesus in a chargeable offense. Their intent was to have him admit that he did not pay imperial tax to Caesar. Mark notes that Herodias, the wife of Herod Antipas the tetrarch of Galilee, was in the group. This Herodias was the one who conspired with her daughter to arrange the execution of John the Baptist. To refute their accusation, Jesus looks at a coin and asks the question, "Whose image is this? And whose inscription?" He then declares, "Give back to Caesar what is Caesar's and to God what is God's." Jesus makes a distinction between the empires of this world and the kingdom of God. He makes it clear that each realm inscribes its image on the resources and the economic processes that belong to it.

1. Whose image is on the people, places, and things around you? Where do you see the image of God? Where do you see the inscription of the Empire?

   • In yourself:

   • In your neighborhood:

   • In your faith community:

2. The economic processes of these two kingdoms operate on distinct narratives. The empires of this world operate on scarcity and greed. The kingdom of God operates on abundance and generosity. Where do you see these two narratives being lived out?

   • In yourself:

   • In your neighborhood:

   • In your faith community:

3. Take some time and make a list of the assets around you. Make a long list, challenging yourself to add things that you may have overlooked in the past. Some of the things you have considered liabilities can become assets when placed in the hands of a generous and creative God.

- Your assets:

- Neighborhood assets:

- Faith community assets:

4. How can you and/or your community leverage these assets to move towards a generosity that looks more like that of Jesus?

5

Small Beginnings

"Never worry about numbers. Help one person at a time and always start with the person nearest you."

MOTHER TERESA

"Better to have a small role in God's story than to cast yourself as the lead in your own fiction."

LECRAE

"The Kingdom of heaven is like a mustard seed."

JESUS

I USED TO THINK bigger was better! And since that was true, it made sense to me that the biggest was the best. I swallowed it—hook, line, and sinker—when people would say, "You must have a God-sized vision! A vision so audacious it would be impossible to accomplish unless God made it happen!" But then I started paying attention to the way Jesus talked about his vision for the future and taking note of the things he valued; it made me reconsider my "bigger is better" perspective. Jesus didn't seem overly concerned about making a big splash or super impressed with grandiose building campaigns.[1] When he told the disciples about his vision to usher in

1. Mark 13:1–2.

God's kingdom on earth and his plan to build a church at the gates of hell,[2] I don't think he thumped his chest and said to Peter, "Go big, or go home!" Instead, he said his kingdom was like a tiny mustard seed, the smallest of all seeds, which would eventually grow and provide shelter for all types of characters.[3] He also compared his vision of the kingdom to a small pinch of yeast that a woman worked into a lump of meal; in secret this invisible kingdom would change the entire culture around it. Eventually the meal would have the same properties as the yeast.[4]

I suppose you could say making Earth look like heaven is a God-sized vision; and it most certainly takes a lot of guts to build a church at the gates of hell. But the way Jesus talked about the kingdom made ordinary people believe they could help make it happen. Jesus insinuated that his vision would work itself out through small, incremental expressions of faithfulness, done over a long period of time. Most of the work would be covert operations, carried out in prayer closets where only God would see, or through small acts of kindness and charity, done behind the scenes where nobody would know about it but God and the one receiving the love.[5]

Once again, as I compare the values of this world to the values of Jesus, there seems to be a big difference between the two. Our world values big things: big TVs, big trucks, big houses, big stores, and megachurches with big TVs. Jesus, on the other hand, seems to value small things. Things like cups of cold water given to little children[6] and small coins given to God by poor widows.[7] Jesus celebrates and blesses people who hunger and thirst for righteousness,[8] he lifts up the meek and says they will inherit the earth,[9] and he loves it when people give themselves to peacemaking. He says they will be called children of God.[10] Jesus values small expressions of righteousness, justice, and peace over and above grand displays of personal achievement.

If a community wants to look like Jesus, they will express God's mercy and peace in humble and meaningful ways. They will persist in well-doing

2. Matt 16:17–19.
3. Luke 13:18–19.
4. Luke 13:20–21.
5. Matt 6:1–6.
6. Matt 10:42.
7. Mark 12:43–44.
8. Matt 5:6.
9. Matt 5:5.
10. Matt 5:9.

even when they feel as if their acts of charity and their pursuit of justice are making little or no impact on the world around them. Rather than giving up, the beloved community will value small beginnings and learn to celebrate the slightest indication of spiritual breakthrough.

Celebrate Small Beginnings

My Twelve-Step friends, who found a home in our Celebrate Recovery program, help me appreciate the importance of celebrating small beginnings. Here's an example of what I mean. A few weeks ago, my kitchen sink broke and I had to call in a plumber to fix it. When he pulled up in front of the house, I couldn't help but notice the sign on the side of his truck. It said, "Fixing the World, One Toilet at a Time." I suppose that's the only way we get anything done—one day at a time, one moment at a time, one step at a time; or, in my plumber's world, one toilet at a time. This world of ours is in such a mess, we can't expect to clean it up with one big flush. It takes what Eugene Peterson calls "a long obedience in the same direction" (which is the title of his classic book on discipleship and spirituality).[11]

My friends in recovery understand the concept of a long obedience in the same direction. They wake up every morning and make a deep and personal commitment to stay clean and sober just for the day. The old-timers in our recovery program tell the newcomers that Celebrate Recovery is a spiritual program and they warn the newcomer, "If you miss the spiritual part of the program, you miss the whole program." They have a wonderful definition for spirituality; they say it's *doing the next right thing over a long period of time.* I guess that's one reason they pray the Serenity Prayer[12] every time they get together:

> God, grant me serenity to accept the things I cannot change, the courage to change the things I can, and the wisdom to know the difference, living one day at a time, enjoying one moment at a time; accepting hardship as a pathway to peace . . .[13]

If we have any hope of changing anything that has gone awry in our world, whether it's a personal character defect that hurts us and those closest to us, or a systemic evil that oppresses and hurts multitudes of people,

---

11. Peterson, *Long Obedience in the Same Direction.*
12. Niebuhr, *Essential Reinhold Niebuhr,* 251.
13. Baker, *Celebrate Recovery,* 236.

the process of change is the same. We pray for courage to change the things we can. We live one day at a time, enjoy one moment at a time, and keep doing the next right thing. We expect pushback from the forces of evil and we accept the hardship as a pathway to peace. To help us persevere we learn to celebrate small beginnings and we applaud little steps made in the right direction.

At the close of every Celebrate Recovery meeting we circle up and hand out tokens to those who have made it another month without relapse. Those who have thirty days of sobriety get a red token. If you make it sixty days you get a green token. The roll call continues: ninety days, six months, nine months—they all receive special recognition, applause, and a colorful token for their accomplishment. When you make it to 365 days we throw a big party. We celebrate like you just returned from walking on the moon.

My favorite token is the blue chip. Every week we give out a blue token for twenty-four hours of sobriety or a desire to make a first step in the right direction. We applaud like a superstar just entered the room and we give bear hugs to anyone who steps up to receive a blue chip. All it takes is one simple step—maybe for some the first step in the right direction—and joy breaks loose in the house. Cheers and high-fives fill the room.

A community that wants to look like Jesus must celebrate any shift that points individuals or moves oppressive systems in a new direction towards personal liberty and social justice.

Our First 365

We've been giving out blue chips every Thursday night for the past nineteen years. That's a lot of chips. But we didn't give out very many during our first year—not because people couldn't make it through twenty-four hours without drinking or drugging. The reason was bleaker than that. We offered the program for twelve months and absolutely no one showed up.

The small group of neighbors, meeting for prayer and worship on Sunday mornings, discerned a felt need in our community. We were certain there was a need for a place and a program that would support our friends who were struggling with compulsive and addictive behaviors. We recruited a small team of twelve people who committed to meet for a year and work through the Celebrate Recovery program. We asked four Sunday school classes from other churches in the city to provide a meal for the people we were planning to serve. Each group volunteered to come one

Thursday night a month for twelve months. After the team was assembled, we rolled up our sleeves and dove in headfirst, excited to offer some help and a little hope to our neighbors who were struggling to overcome their hurts, habits, and hang-ups.

The Celebrate Recovery program takes a year to complete. Every month you work through two lessons and you hear two testimonies from people in recovery. Week after week we met and waited for our neighbors to come and join us. Week after week we sat in a circle by ourselves and took turns teaching the lesson or sharing our testimony. We heard each other's story twice in the first year and pretended on the second go-round we were hearing it for the first time. If a visitor did wander in, the twelve of us would overwhelm them with enthusiasm. Some returned for a second visit, but most were too afraid to come back. I think they decided they would rather drink than endure our giddy hospitality.

The final months of the year were beyond discouraging; it was embarrassing to have volunteer cooks drive across town to feed the twelve of us. In December we had to make a decision: throw in the towel or keep trudging? We felt certain God was leading us to offer the program, but from all logical measurements our effort was a dismal failure. I was ready to call it quits and would have, but one of the twelve read a verse of Scripture from Zechariah: "Do not despise these small beginnings, for the Lord rejoices to see the work begin."[14] Others on the team insisted that God wanted us to keep meeting. The volunteer cooks enlisted for another year, and all twelve team members signed up to share their testimony a third time.

Becki had been a part of the team from the beginning and volunteered to lead us during the second year. Having a leader from the neighborhood that knew firsthand the devastating effects of alcoholism made all the difference. Becki was the person of peace that made the connection between our neighbors who struggled with addictive behaviors and the hope offered at Celebrate Recovery. She went to A.A. meetings around the city and invited everyone she met to the eating-meeting on Thursday night, where children were welcome and cared for, and Christ was celebrated as the higher power. She went to the sober living houses scattered around the west end of our city and invited the residents to our weekly celebration. She even paid a visit to one of our local prisons and told the inmates she met, "When you get paroled, come and visit us at Celebrate Recovery." It was a

14. Zech 4:10.

pleasant surprise when Bill showed up one Thursday night and thanked God for sending Becki to the prison where he had been incarcerated.

Shortly after Bill was paroled, he landed a job at Our Father's House, a sober living house in the neighborhood. Every week for the next ten years, Bill brought a busload of men to Celebrate Recovery. Whenever Bill shared his story, he would thank God for sending an angel to visit him in prison. Finding his way to Celebrate Recovery and stepping up to get a blue chip was his first step in a new direction. Bill never forgot the difference that one step made in his life.

Looking back, I realize how easy it would have been for the twelve of us to call it quits after the first year. No one would have blamed us. However, if we had stopped meeting because of low attendance, we would have never met Bill and all of his friends from Our Father's House. Our church family, and the DNA that makes us who we are, would look and feel a lot different today without the family members we've gathered through our Celebrate Recovery connection.

The inspiration we discovered in Zechariah gave us the tenacity and the will to do the next right thing. When you set out to follow Jesus and build community around his values, never despise small beginnings. On the contrary, celebrate the small stuff.

BHAGS versus Small Giants

Setting your focus on small is outrageous! And blatantly countercultural! So much so, it feels wrong to write it down or to say it out loud. In almost every profession, leaders are trained to think big and to chase after exponential growth. The "bigger is better" paradigm drives our culture. It doesn't matter if you're working in the business world, the church world, or coaching little league—leaders are challenged to be the best. Don't hear me saying there's something wrong with giving our best. As a matter of fact, I'm in favor of it. The problem arises when "best" gets translated "biggest" or being the one on top when the game is over.

When our denominational leaders discovered we were "doing church" in the chapel of the after-school community center, they suggested I join an incubator for church planters. I had never heard of such a thing before—an incubator for church planters sounded weird. I soon discovered *incubator* was a rather popular term in corporate America. We church folk like to take our cues for leadership from gurus in the corporate world. There's nothing wrong with learning best practices from leaders of corporations; however, we risk losing focus on vocational identity and purpose if we listen more intently to corporate leaders than to prophetic leaders from our faith tradition. But like I said, joining an incubator sounded weird, so I gave it a whirl.

The first book on our reading list was a book called *Good to Great,* written by Jim Collins. It was a fascinating book. My personal review would place it somewhere between a good read and a great read. The research and accumulated data was mind-blowing. His team of researchers studied twenty-eight companies that transitioned from privately owned companies to publicly owned. From the group of twenty-eight companies, they identified eleven "good-to-great" companies that sustained cumulative stock returns three times the market over fifteen years. The eleven "good-to-great" companies were compared to the other eighteen companies that failed to make or sustain similar returns. Collins was looking for what great companies shared in common that distinguished them from the comparison companies.

Collins's team of researchers identified six key concepts that distinguished the "good-to-great" companies from the "mediocre." Their list included: effective leadership qualities, team building principles, brutally honest evaluation processes, cultures of discipline, and using technology as a way to accelerate effectiveness.[15] All of these are great leadership qualities for any organization, including small missional communities. But the concept that captured the attention of my incubator was what Collins identified as the BHAG principle (Big Hairy Audacious Goals.)[16] After we read the book, the entire group was mesmerized and thought every church ought to have a BHAG.

For church planters, *big, hairy, and audacious* usually refers to a grandiose goal for attendance at the Sunday morning worship service. Or having a collective mass of people affirm the audacious goal of winning the whole world for Jesus. It was a no-brainer for my incubator coach: if your goal was *big* enough and *hairy* enough, you would be on your way to leading a Fortune 500 Church. I couldn't quite put my finger on it, but there was something about our obsession with the BHAG concept that didn't ring true.

The suspicion was accentuated when we went on field trips. Our denomination likes to send new church planters around the country to visit

15. Collins, *Good to Great,* 5–8.
16. Collins, *Good to Great,* 197–204.

our "flagship" churches—megachurches that are doing big, hairy, and audacious things. The field trips never inspired me. I always came home to my thirty-something community feeling like a failure. "Thirty-something" was not our median age demographic; it was our average attendance.

Thirty people, sitting in a circle, drinking coffee and reading Scripture, lacked luster when compared to the big hairy churches. I remember going to a church planting conference that made a big deal about exponential growth. My colleagues attended workshops like "Breaking the Three-Hundred Barrier"; others went to a workshop called "Breaking the Five-Hundred Barrier." I searched the brochure from cover to cover, but never found a workshop on "Breaking the Thirty Barrier." If I ever go back to one of those church growth conferences I'm going to ask if I can lead a workshop. I'm going to call it "Breaking Barriers with the Thirty People You Have."

About halfway through the incubator process, I started to get a chip on my shoulder. I was frustrated and bored. All the big to-do over church growth principles didn't fit with our experience in Portland. I decided it would be better for my emotional health to quit going on the "incubator" field trips—they were incubating something we didn't want to hatch.

Right after I swore off the "Go and See" visits to megachurches, I was invited to a Fresh Expressions workshop. The brochure about this particular workshop told me "Fresh Expressions was an international movement of missionary disciples cultivating new kinds of church alongside existing congregations to more effectively engage our growing post-Christian society."[17] The description of the group piqued my curiosity. I signed up with a bit of begrudging respect, hopeful to hear something new, *fresh,* and relevant to our context. The guy leading the learning experience normalized church planting for me. He told us the average size of a new church plant hovered around fifty people. And then he said, "If you make *mission* the organizing principle for the church, you may find your average attendance smaller still." It was refreshing to hear someone suggest that the matrix you set to measure the success of your community needs to be in alignment with your values and the mission of the community. His words were like music to my ears. The metaphor of *big, hairy, and audacious* was set free. It no longer meant big numbers. Our leadership team was empowered to make big, hairy, and audacious goals around acts of service and expressions of love for God and love for our neighbors.

---

17. https://freshexpressionsus.org/about/#what, lines 3–4.

The Fresh Expressions workshop inspired me to rethink the good-to-great BHAG concept. The simple and plain truth is this: big does not equal great, nor does small mean mediocre! Size is not the point. Holding tight to this principle helps our beloved community remain faithful to our values and stay true to our mission.

The paradigm shift towards big-does-not-equal-great was reinforced when I made a fundraising visit to a potential donor. The chairman of our board had a friend who owned a bank. He wanted to introduce me to his friend so I could ask him for a big, hairy, audacious donation. We set aside a day to travel across the state to a small, rural town in central Kentucky. On the way to our meeting, I had to mentally prepare myself. I had never met anyone who owned a bank before. I assumed the guy would be a bit pompous—owning a bank and all. But I was totally taken off guard. This guy was excited about life. He loved Jesus and he loved people. He was curious about my work and the little church of thirty-something people we had in Portland. He wanted to hear about the children and the teenagers in our after-school program. We talked, and laughed, and listened to each other's stories, and then he handed me a book called *Small Giants*, written by Bo Burlingham. I couldn't believe the subtitle of the book: *Companies That Choose to Be Great Instead of Big*.

Much as with Collins's book, Burlingham researched great companies that were singled out for their extraordinary achievement by other companies in their own industries or by independent observers.[18] However, Burlingham focused his research on "privately owned companies that were willing to forego revenue or geographic growth, if necessary, in order to achieve other remarkable ends."[19] The shareholders who owned the businesses in his book had other non-financial priorities in addition to their financial objectives. They were interested in being great at what they did, creating a great place to work, providing great service to customers, having great relationships with their suppliers, making great contributions to the communities where they lived and worked, and finding great ways to lead their lives. The owners of the companies knew that if they wanted to excel in all of these other areas, they had to keep ownership and control inside the company and in many cases, place significant limits on how much and how fast they grew.[20]

18. Burlingham, *Small Giants*, xx.

19. Burlingham, *Small Giants*, xix.

20. Burlingham, *Small Giants*, xvii.

With the book sitting in my lap, my new friend began to share a little more of his story. There was a point in time when his family considered going public with their bank. He said, "If we had, we could have made a bundle of money, moved the corporation to one of the larger cities in the state, and built a high-rise tower." But they decided to grow in a different direction—a direction they felt honored the values of Jesus better. My new friend and his family decided if they remained in control of the bank, and the profits, they could leverage their resources in ways that would benefit the small town where they grew up.

After our meeting, we took a walk down Main Street. At every corner we paused long enough for my new friend to point out the historic buildings his bank had renovated. Community-owned businesses, supported through the bank's community trust fund, now occupied the once abandoned buildings. My new friend's bank was a small giant. Rather than go public and become enslaved to shareholders' demands for a steady increase in profits and market shares, his family made a conscious decision to stay small so they could do great things in their community. This family's decision put a new spin on the phrase "Go big, or go home." Sometimes going home and doing great things, instead of going big, is the best thing to do!

Rethinking Greatness

Jesus made some decisions early in his public ministry that appear to be motivated by this "small giant" principle. First off, whenever Jesus healed people, he instructed them to keep it on the down-low. He didn't want people telling others that he had the power to do miraculous things. Second, when Jesus was presented with an opportunity to go big and increase his social platform, he decided to keep the community he was investing in small.

In the first chapter of Mark's Gospel we watch as Jesus gets baptized and begins to build his leadership team. Before the close of chapter one, Jesus announces, "The kingdom of God has come near."[21] He performs a few miracles, heals a number of people, and casts out some evil spirits. Mark says that "news about him spread quickly over the whole region of Galilee."[22]

21. Mark 1:15.
22. Mark 1:28.

On one particular day, Jesus heals Simon's mother-in-law from a fever. As soon as the fever breaks, she gets out of bed and prepares a meal for everybody. The word gets out. "Something extraordinary is going down at Simon's house! His mom is cooking up a storm and a man named Jesus is healing people!" The neighbors start showing up at the doorstep. Mark says that by sundown "the whole town gathered at the door, and Jesus healed many who had various diseases."[23]

Publicity was circulating, a collective mass of people had been gathered, the location was set, teaching and pastoral care were being provided. From a church-growth perspective, it was time to brand the church, design the logo, and print the t-shirts. But Jesus had something greater in mind than building a consumer-based local church that trafficked in religious goods and services. He was more interested in planting seeds that would one day grow into a kingdom movement.

Mark says, "Very early in the morning, while it was still dark, Jesus got up, left the house and went off to a solitary place [to pray]."[24] Later that morning, Simon and his friends went out to find Jesus, to let him know that "everyone" was looking for him. The way Mark tells the story, you get the feeling Simon was surprised to hear that Jesus was ready to move on to another location. Why in the world would he slip off and leave such an enthusiastic crowd behind?

Instead of settling for big, Jesus went after great. He traveled throughout Galilee, preaching about the kingdom of God, healing the sick, and delivering people from oppressive forces of evil. His personality was a rare and unique mix of humility and power. His humble authority and the way he spoke truth to power amazed some and threatened others. These character traits, combined with his compassion towards the sick and the oppressed set him apart as a *great* prophetic and spiritual leader.

As he and his friends traveled from one place to the next, he took every opportunity he could to teach his small base of followers about the kingdom of God and to train them how to do the things he was doing. It was his way of seeding movemental constructs and missional DNA into the leadership culture of the community he was forming. Staying small gave him the freedom to invest deeply in a select group of people, cultivating a few *great* leaders to carry out his mission and vision for the future.

23. Mark 1:34.
24. Mark 1:35.

As Jesus and his small band of potential leaders wandered across the countryside, he discussed with them, on more than one occasion, their aspirations for greatness. The first conversation happened while they were in a town called Capernaum. Mark tells the story this way:

> When [Jesus] was in the house, he asked them, "What were you arguing about on the Road?" But they kept quiet because on the way they had argued about who was the greatest. Sitting down, Jesus called the Twelve and said, "If anyone wants to be first, he must be the very last, and the servant of all."[25]

A second conversation about greatness follows close on the heels of this story—only one chapter later. Either these friends of Jesus were slow learners, or Mark repeats the story to make his point loud and clear: *in the way of Jesus, greatness is achieved through humility and service.*

On this second occasion, James and John, the sons of Zebedee, ask Jesus for a special favor. They want to be granted positions of power and privilege: "Let one of us sit at your right and the other at your left in your glory."[26] When the other ten guys caught wind of their scheme of self-aggrandizement, they were furious. Mark says they were "indignant." Jesus doesn't scold them or shame anyone for their aspirations to be great; rather, he leverages each opportunity to redefine greatness and explain what it looks like in the kingdom of heaven:

> You know that those who are regarded as rulers of the Gentiles lord it over them, and their high officials exercise authority over them. Not so with you. Instead, whoever wants to become great among you must be your servant, and whoever wants to be first must be slave of all. For even the Son of Man did not come to be served, but to serve, and to give his life as a ransom for many.[27]

In his book, *Practicing Greatness*, Reggie McNeal reflects on these two stories and makes this observation:

> In neither discussion does Jesus disparage the ambition to be great. Nor does he float the idea of greatness as something his follower-leaders might aspire to. Rather, he takes it for granted that their motivations would push them toward achieving greatness. He just wants to point them in the right direction. He seizes the moment

25. Mark 9:33–35.
26. Mark 10:37.
27. Mark 10:42–45.

to contrast the prevailing notions of greatness with the genuine article and to challenge them to see greatness in spiritual terms. Jesus' idea of greatness revolves around humility and service—a far cry from our typical association with this concept.[28]

If the path to greatness in the kingdom of God is a journey towards humility and service, we have a critical need in our current church culture to produce a new breed of great spiritual leaders—men and women who will take a pass on power, position, and privilege, choosing instead to lead beloved communities in the way of Jesus. The small giant principle may be a much-needed key to help the church find its way forward in our current postmodern context. I believe a new variety of free-flowing networks of micromissional communities—that embrace the radical, upside-down values of Jesus—are needed to lead the church into the future. These small giants will be able to influence neighborhoods and cities with kingdom values in ways not attainable to large-membership churches with regional-sprawl congregations. If we have any notion of creating such a community, we will value small beginnings, celebrate the slightest indication of spiritual breakthrough, and set our matrix for greatness around humble acts of service.

The Big Problem of Poverty

There's another reason small beginnings are important to Jesus, and should be honored by those who choose to follow him. When we fall in love with Jesus and allow him to take center stage, we will long to give ourselves to what he called "the more important matters of the law: justice, mercy, and faithfulness."[29] However, as soon as we set our face towards these weightier matters, the complexity of our globalized world will overwhelm us. You can rest assured the question will arise, *How can one person or one community make a difference*? How you answer the question is why small beginnings are so important.

Social evil and its unrelenting web of oppressive systems can dissuade the most caring and loving people, convincing them to throw up their hands and do nothing in the name of futility. Consider for a moment a few of the pressing social issues facing our world today: global poverty, a broken criminal justice system, the need for a humane immigration process,

28. McNeal, *Practicing Greatness*, 3.
29. Matt 23:23.

the urgent need for ecological restoration, national economies built on war, racism. Take any one of these issues, set your heart on making a difference, and you'll soon discover it is interrelated with all the other issues on a global scale. The question intensifies—*How can one person or one small community make a difference?*

The number of people who exist under the foreboding weight of poverty is unthinkable. Ten percent of the world's population—more than 730 million of our brothers and sisters—lives in extreme poverty, earning less than $1.90 a day.[30] The weight of global poverty increases when you consider the fact that more than one billion people don't have access to safe and clean water, creating an unhealthy environment where children die. In 2019 alone, 7.4 million children and young people under the age of 25 died largely due to treatable causes such as infectious diseases and sanitation-related illnesses.[31] It is impossible for me to imagine the gnawing pain associated with this deep level of poverty.

When I zoom in closer to home and consider the economic disparity within the boarders of the wealthiest country in the history of the world, I shake my head in disbelief. In the United States of America, 38.1 million people live below the poverty line and 27.5 million people don't have access to adequate health care or insurance.[32] In the land of the free and the home of the brave, over 550,000 people go homeless every night, sleeping on the streets or in emergency shelters.[33] These are more than numbers; they are neighbors—our brothers and our sisters.

These statistics are daunting. Far too many Christians look at the big problem of poverty from a distance and decide that one person can't make a difference. Rather than take Jesus seriously and embrace his value of small beginnings, they take a quick glance at the problem and then look the other way. Feelings of guilt are easily resolved by saying, "One small community can't shift the convoluted network of imperial systems that perpetuate poverty, so we'll shift our focus to something a little more gratifying . . . like ourselves."

But when a community dares to believe in the mustard seed faith of Jesus, another scenario begins to unfold. The community will be inspired by the Spirit of God to express kingdom values in simple and creative ways.

---

30. "Eleven Facts about Global Poverty," lines 1, 7–9.

31. UNICEF, "Levels and Trends in Child Mortality," lines 1, 4–6.

32. Fessler, "U. S. Census Bureau," lines 8–10, 13–14.

33. National Alliance to End Homelessness, "State of Homelessness," lines 7–9.

Small expressions of what Jesus considered "the more important matters of the law" will become prophetic examples of how life is intended to be lived—evidence of a hope born in heaven that stands in contradiction to the way things are on earth. These expressions of justice, mercy, and faithfulness will offer hope to the hopeless and proclaim truth and judgment to evil systems that oppress the poor. If we believe in the power of the mustard seed, the possibilities of making a difference in our world are limitless. Simple acts of mercy, speaking up and speaking out to advocate for the poor, leveraging our social and material capital on behalf of the poor, civil demonstrations, and prophetic works of art that cause others to pause and consider the injustice of poverty, are small ways we can let the world know that our beloved community does indeed stand in solidarity with the poor.

Beloved communities that embrace the value of small beginnings will understand the enormous power and eternal significance of befriending the poor. When the poor are no longer a social problem to be solved or a social justice issue to discuss with your progressive friends over coffee, you may discover a friendship that leads you deeper into the heart of Jesus. When the rich befriend the poor, they meet Jesus on Jesus' terms. After all, it was Jesus who said, "When you welcome the poor, you welcome me." Humble relationships that cross socioeconomic barriers will demonstrate to the world that the kingdom of heaven is near and will reveal what heaven looks like on earth—a diverse community where everyone shares equal value. Authentic reconciling relationships that bridge socioeconomic barriers accomplish more than you might imagine. They create opportunity for the poor to be empowered and for the rich to be freed from the idolatrous grip of materialism.

If you think the problem of poverty is too big, then I urge you to do something small. Don't compare your contribution to others. Don't evaluate your gift merely on the impact it makes on the big problem; and by all means, don't let the enormity of the problem dissuade you from stepping into the mess. Just do the next right thing. Your humble expression of compassion will be noticed by God and will be used as a prophetic demonstration of faithfulness. You will be investing yourself in the weightier matters of justice and mercy.

Promise Housing Plus

A few years ago, my son Ryan purchased a home in the neighborhood. He bought what some of his friends called "a real fixer-upper." Others called it a dump. I distinctly remember the first day we walked through the house. In the far reaches of his imagination Ryan saw potential. My imagination couldn't reach that far. In every room and down the hallway, we stepped over piles of trash left behind by the previous owner, who had moved out ten years earlier. On top of the trash left by the former owner was another layer of junk, left behind by a decade of squatters who occupied the house to manufacture drugs. I forced a smile as Ryan said, "All the place needs is a little tender loving care." Behind the fake smile, I was thinking, "This place needs a lot more than a little TLC!" It needed plumbing, electricity, a new roof, new windows and doors, new walls, new paint, hard work and a ton of sweat. Ryan only paid $6,000 for the house. Somewhere between cleaning out all the trash and patching the holes in the roof, Ryan decided he paid $4,000 too much. A year later, the potential he saw while looking at the heap of garbage blossomed into a beautifully restored historic home in Portland.

It wasn't long until Ryan began to wonder if he could do it again. Could he use his newfound skill in home renovation and his passion for community development to create an affordable home for one of his neighbors? His vision was simple: create a construction company called Promise Housing Plus. Remodel one house, help one neighbor become a homeowner, and employ one person from the neighborhood. If it worked he would do it again the next year.

A few friends of the church heard about Ryan's plan and offered to help. They were faithful donors to the church and loved to help whenever they could. They came up with a brilliant idea. Instead of giving their annual donation directly to the church, as they had been doing, they invested their money in Promise Housing. When Ryan was ready to sell the house to one of our neighbors, the new homeowner would make their monthly mortgage payment to the church.

When I add up the community benefit affected by this economic stream I count several bottom lines. One, the community has a newly renovated historic home that had been slated by the city for demolition. You can imagine the condition of the house when you realize Ryan bought the house from the city for one dollar. Two, after the renovation was complete he sold the house at an affordable price to our neighbor Amanda, who moved to Portland a few years before to live in a transitional house for women in crisis. Now Amanda has a stable place to live, a home in which to raise her son, and an opportunity to build personal wealth through home ownership. Three, Ryan hired his friend Ben to help on the renovation project. Ben is a gifted craftsman who moved to Portland to live for a season in a sober-living house. Now Ben has a job he loves and he plays a vital role in our community—building homes for others and helping his friends in recovery rebuild their lives. Four, the missional church receives a monthly income stream, spread out over several years. Five, the donor gets a quadruple win for their gift and Ryan gets to keep the lights on at the house he built for his family.

Promise Housing Plus is a great example of a small, yet creative expression of kingdom economics, in response to the big problem of poverty. I wonder what could happen if the mustard seed idea of Promise Housing was reproduced in other cities. Think about the enormous amount of charitable gifts given each year to local churches around the country; is it possible to create a process where financial contributions, given to support the budget of local churches, could be leveraged to meet other social needs on their way to the church coffers? When you believe in the power of small beginnings, the possibilities of blessing others with God's good and abundant resources are limitless.

Small Beginnings on Baird Street

From time to time, I forget how valuable small beginnings really are. When that happens, I try to recall the benchmarks we celebrated during those early days on Baird Street. In those days we only had nineteen boys and girls in the children's after-school program, and a youth group with six middle-school girls, and Ronnie. The children would fight every day—about anything and everything! If we made it through a day without a fight, Kathie and I would go home and celebrate the small measure of success.

The fight I remember best went down during our first Christmas pageant. Nada, Nikki, and Ronnie were assigned to be shepherds and given bathrobes as costumes. Desiree and David were cast as the Holy Family, with similar costumes. Their bathrobes included tinsel wrapped around a coat hanger, to be worn as a halo. I had no clue how coveted the role was until dress rehearsal. Right after the angels finished singing "O Little Town of Bethlehem," the Three Wise Men came running into the house with their hands waving in the air, screaming, "The shepherds are beating up Mother Mary and Joseph!"

The children didn't need a legitimate reason to fight, it was just part of life. It was the way they expressed every emotion. Mad, sad, glad, or afraid . . . they were all expressed the same. By fighting! When the middle-school girls were jealous, they would call each other names. When they were mad, they would choose sides, go out back and fight. When they were happy and all was going well, they would beat up Ronnie.

Whenever a new boy came by the Center, the girls would flirt by throwing rocks at the new kid and chase him down the street, swinging sticks in the air. In desperation to get some teenage boys to come and stay, I put up a basketball hoop in the parking lot. Soon the number of boys who were able to endure the brutal assault of rocks and sticks increased. The summer after the Holy Family got jumped we had enough young boys to play a pick-up game of basketball. That fall they asked if they could play in the church basketball league. It was a small beginning, worthy of celebration. But the celebration was short-lived. Later that night, I thought about the way they talked to each other on the basketball court and realized they'd be thrown out of the league before half time of the first game.

The next day we gathered in my furnace room/office, for a man-to-man talk. I told the boys trash talk wouldn't be allowed. If they wanted to play in the church league they would have to refrain from cursing on the court. You would have thought I said they had to play ball with one hand tied behind their back. They moaned and laughed all at the same time. Little Kev was the first to speak: "Larry, you don't get it, we can't play ball if we can't talk trash! We're gonna lose every game. That's how we play!" Wayne stood up and shouted, "How we play? That's why we play!" More laughter filled the air, seasoned with a few more of their favorite curse words.

Together, we came up with a creative solution. I told the boys to make a list with all the inappropriate words and derogatory names they could think of. Once the list was complete, they would assign a number to every word on the list; from then on whenever they felt the need to talk trash they could yell out their favorite number instead. They could even say it with attitude! We laughed, a few cursed, and then they headed to the parking lot to make their list.

A week later, a volunteer named Kay came by to help Wanda with her homework. As she passed the furnace room she peeked in and asked, "Why are the boys outside yelling numbers at each other?" I smiled and shrugged my shoulders. Kay smiled and with a puzzled look on her face, mumbled something about "teenagers these days." When she was out of sight I grabbed my Nerf basketball and did a little dance, ending with a slam-dunk on the plastic rim attached to the back of my office door. It was a small beginning that called for a celebration!

Playing ball in a church league and learning to think before you talk trash was a small drop in the bucket of skill sets my young friends needed to learn. The truth is, it didn't change anything in the scope of all that was wrong in their world. But it was a good and positive step in the right direction. When the next season rolled around the basketball team began to join Kay and Wanda in the tutoring room.

Now and then, when I'm planting flowers in the spring, or raking leaves in the fall, thinking about how swiftly another year has passed, one of the young men or young women from those early days on Baird Street will see me in the yard and we'll take a little time to reminisce. In one way or another, they express their gratitude for all the people who worked or volunteered at the church, creating a safe place where they could learn and play after school. Many of them will say, "If it hadn't been for the church, no telling where I would have wound up." The conversations will fast forward to the present, and they'll tell me about their job or show me pictures of their children. It makes for a good day when I hear things are going well for one of my young friends from way back when. It reminds me that small steps in the right direction add up to a good life.

There is one particular success story from those early days on Baird Street that I love to tell every chance I get—the story about Wanda and Kay's friendship. Wanda was one of the original members in our College Connection program. The program matched adult mentors with children in the fourth grade. The mentors committed to meet with and encourage the students during the school year. Every year, the College Connection students went on field trips to universities and colleges around the country. They got to sit in on college classes, eat in the college cafeterias, and meet with college students to ask them about college life. Year after year, the students in the program were encouraged to explore things they were interested in and to dream about their future. To help encourage their dreams we created a scholarship endowment fund for the students to access when they graduated from high school and we asked them every week, starting in the fourth grade, "What year will you graduate from college?"

Kay tutored and mentored Wanda all the way through her elementary, middle-, and high-school career. However, Kay was far more than Wanda's tutor. She was more than a mentor. Kay and Wanda became the best of friends. When Wanda graduated from high school, she invited her friend Kay to the graduation celebration. Four years later, when Wanda graduated from college, she returned home and got a job teaching at the elementary school in the neighborhood.

A generation later, Wanda now volunteers her time at the Center, befriending other children the way Kay befriended her. Wanda spends her life helping children cultivate a passion for education. Every day, she creates a safe place for kids to learn and play. She celebrates the small accomplishments they make and she encourages them to dream about the future. Wanda knows her students can grow into their dreams, if they simply do the next right thing over a long period of time.

A life well lived, is a life filled with small expressions of love.
I think that's why Jesus valued small beginnings and teaches those who
follow him to do the same.

RED LETTER QUESTIONS

Who is greater, the one who is at the table or the one who serves?

In Luke 22:24–30, the disciples have a dispute about which one of them is the greatest. Jesus settles their dispute by asking a question: "Who is greater, the one who is at the table or the one who serves? Is it not the one who is at the table? But I am among you as one who serves." Jesus does not rebuke his friends for wanting to be great; he simply redefines the connotation of greatness.

1. Read the story and consider these questions:

   - What does it mean to be great in the world's eyes?

   - What does it mean to be great in the kingdom of God?

2. Take the next week and begin a needs assessment of your neighborhood. Consider the following suggestions to help make the assessment:

   - Visit with your neighbors and conduct interviews to hear from them.

   - Host a community forum with round-table discussions. Have each table list the top ten needs in the neighborhood and report out to the larger group. Prioritize the list.

   - Interview city officials, local leaders, service providers, and teachers.

   - What is taking place (or not taking place) in your neighborhood that disturbs you the most?

3. When passion and assets intersect with public need there is an invitation for a missional response. Recall the list of assets and resources you made in the last chapter. How can those assets and your passion be leveraged to meet one need listed in your needs assessment?

6

New Beginnings

"Forgiveness says you are given another chance to make a new beginning."
DESMOND TUTU

*"I do not at all understand the mystery of grace—only that it meets us
where we are but does not leave us where it found us."*
ANNE LAMOTT

"Even if they sin against you seven times in a day and *seven times* come
back to you saying 'I repent,' you must forgive them."
JESUS

WHEN WE HIT THE fifteen-year mark of living and working in the neighborhood, we found ourselves in the middle of an interpersonal implosion. In 2005, the Promise Center purchased an abandoned warehouse down the street from our main facility, with plans to create a worship center that would function as an economic development hub for the neighborhood. The vision was exciting, resources were coming in, and new staff members were joining the community. We were hiring staff from the neighborhood and Christian families were choosing to relocate to Portland.

We were living the dream . . . and then 2008 happened. The Great Recession dried up the economic streams supporting the vision. The

warehouse dream soon became a nightmare. Even though financial resources were scarce, there was no shortage on blame.

In addition to the financial woes, I made some leadership decisions
and staff hires that didn't sit well with other team members. People began
to leave the community. Some silently quit supporting the work; others became vocally critical. We experienced a hurtful and harmful break in community. The deepest hurt was no doubt the relationships that were severed.
Words of forgiveness were spoken, but reconciliation never happened. The
broken relationships left harmful scars on our witness and scars of grief on
the hearts of all the families directly involved. It was a long dark night of
the soul for all of us.

It is one thing for a program idea to go down the tubes or for a building campaign to fizzle; failures such as these may bruise the ego or become
a source of embarrassment. But it is quite another matter when leaders in
the church experience a break in community. Faction in Christian community feels more like malpractice than failure. The heartbeat of Christian
ministry is a call to reconciliation—reconciling people to God and to one
another.[1] Our failed attempt to model reconciliation for our neighbors
continues to be the saddest part of my time in Portland. The shadow cast
by this season of failure was difficult to integrate with the light of joyful
community that preceded the break. Our hope of creating a beloved community was deferred and the proverb proved true: hope deferred dries up
the bones.[2] In spite of our dried bones and sick heart, God used this season
of failure to clarify our values and to renew our community's commitment
to the neighborhood. In time, we found the grace to pick up the pieces, we
learned from our mistakes, and we stepped into a new beginning.

The Value of New Beginnings

The way of Jesus is the way of extravagant grace and new beginnings. Consider for a moment the conversation Jesus had with Peter on the topic of
forgiveness. Peter's question was sincere; he thought he was being more
than generous and extremely gracious. "Lord, how many times shall I forgive my brother or sister who sins against me? Up to seven times?" Peter
had no idea how deeply Jesus valued forgiveness and new beginnings. Jesus

1. 2 Cor 5:11–21.
2. Prov 13:12.

answered Peter, "I tell you not seven times, but seventy-seven times."[3] It was his way of saying: *We will forgive those who sin against us an infinite amount of times.* Grace, Jesus-style, will create a culture that values mercy over judgment, forgiveness over shame, and freedom over bondage. Rather than harboring resentments, which limits the potential for new life, a community built on the values of Jesus will be known for its extravagant grace. The courage to explore new beginnings will be unconstrained!

Not only does Jesus value forgiveness and new beginnings, they stand apart as two of God's supreme gifts to humanity. The prophets, the psalmist, and the passion of Christ all point in the same direction—God loves to take our failures and turn them into beautiful expressions of new life!

For example, during the Assyrian exile, when Judah's failure as a nation could not be covered up or denied, Jeremiah encouraged his peers by saying, "Because of the Lord's great love we are not consumed, for his compassions never fail. They are new every morning."[4] Every sunrise, says Jeremiah, is a reminder of God's grace. The failures of yesterday need not determine our future.

Isaiah speaks similar words of encouragement to Israel during the Babylonian exile: "Do not remember the former things, nor consider the things of old. See, I am doing a new thing! Now it springs up; do you not perceive it? I am making a way in the wilderness and streams in the wasteland."[5] Whenever personal or corporate failure lands us—or the community we love—in desolate places, we can rest assured God is willing and able to create a way out of the wilderness. Former mistakes should not prevent us from moving forward into new ways of being. When Isaiah tells Israel to forget the former things, he is not suggesting they pretend their moral failure didn't happen. If we fail to learn from our failures, we are prone to repeat them in the future. Isaiah has already called the nation to account regarding their part in the exile, to learn from their mistakes, and to readjust their beliefs and their behavior. Now he is inviting the nation to see what God is able to do in spite of their national blunder.

Many of the Psalms carry the same theme—God's grace cancels the wages of sin and creates a pathway to new life. I love how the psalmists acknowledge the full range of human emotion. They don't pull any punches or sugarcoat the human experience. The Psalms are jam-packed with

3. Matt 18:21–22.

4. Lam 3:22–24a.

5. Isa 43:19.

poems and prayers that deal with love and revenge, confidence and fear, joy and sorrow, praise and lament, victory and failure. The cord that runs through every psalm, with their wide array of human experience, is hope. In spite of our failures and in the face of our greatest fears—whether they are brought on by our own character defect, an innocent mistake, or some circumstance beyond our control—we can place our hope in God's faithfulness. God can and will take our failures, along with the subsequent sorrow of heart, and transform them into an instrument of joy. The Psalms teach us to sing, "God's favor lasts a lifetime; weeping may stay for the night, but rejoicing comes in the morning."[1] Once we internalize God's gift of grace and realize the great value Jesus places on forgiveness and new beginnings, we, like the psalmist, will have a firm foundation on which to place our hope.

For hope to be more than a whimsical dream or a fleeting last-ditch effort to change our circumstance with positive thinking, we need a solid, historical foundation on which to place our hope. From the Judeo-Christian perspective, God's promises in Scripture and God's acts in history provide such a ground. God's initiative in and through the life of Jesus is our foundation for hope. In the life, death, and resurrection of Jesus, God confronts evil and human failure with creative power and extravagant grace. God gave God's best to the world—God's own son. In response to God's good gift, humanity did its worst. The world rejected the gift and crucified the Son of God. The mind-boggling phenomenon of the Christian story is the fact that God took humanity's moral failure and transformed it into the salvation of the world. Through the death and resurrection of Jesus, God met our failure with grace and transformed the crucifixion of Jesus into a place of forgiveness and new beginnings. God made a way for us to live abundant and free lives. Because of God's great love for us, demonstrated in the Easter story, we are free to live and love. We can take risks, and when we fail, we have a place to turn. At the foot of the cross we can find forgiveness, renew our faith, and begin again.

Free to Fail

I believe Jesus would prefer we live our dreams and fail rather than play it safe and never live.[2] The only way to dodge failure is to never take risk, never become vulnerable, never invest in a dream, never take a shot at love,

1. Ps 30:5.
2. Matt 25:14–30.

isolate ourselves, and play it safe. Unfortunately, an insular and sterile life free from the risk of failure is no life at all; in the end, we fail at what matters most—life itself.

I believe most sane people will avoid failure at all cost; however, not everyone operates with a sane mind. Some people embrace failure as a necessary step on the pathway to success. It was Charles Kettering, a twentieth-century inventor, who said: "Every great improvement has come after repeated failures. Virtually nothing comes out right the first time. Failures, repeated failures, are finger posts on the road to achievement. One fails forward toward success."[3] Leaders and entrepreneurs on the cutting edge of innovation appreciate the function of failure and they value new beginnings. Their logic goes like this: the faster you fail, the faster you'll find your way to success.[4]

This same logic holds true for communities of faith. A beloved community that meets failure with grace and embraces the value of new beginnings will create an environment where people are encouraged to dream and explore new ways of organizing their community to better fulfill its mission. If a new strategy goes belly-up, the community will make amends when necessary, learn from its mistakes, and grow in wisdom. In the wake of the failure, rather than yield to the voice that says, "We tried that once and it didn't work," or "We never did it that way before," it will reflect on the failure, adapt, and reimagine the next right thing.

History books are filled with creative thinkers who understood the vital relationship between failure and new beginnings—people like Henry Ford, who said, "Failure is the opportunity to begin again more intelligently."[5] Or Thomas Edison, who reframed failure by saying, "I have not failed. I've just found 10,000 ways that won't work."[6] When failure is seen as a necessary step on the pathway to success, creativity is reinforced. Dreamers are free to dream. Pioneers are free to explore. In the process, these stargazing entrepreneurs will lead the community into new and more fruitful ways of meeting their objectives.

3. Kettering, "Science Quotes," lines 15–16.
4. Kittle, "Succeed Fast, by Failing Faster."
5. Ford and Crowther, *My Life and Work*, 19–20.
6. Edison, "Thomas Edison Quotes," lines 1–2.

Colorectal Theology

When a community operates in a culture of grace, where new beginnings are valued, people will be encouraged to chase after their passions. Working hand in hand and cheering one another on in spite of failures and setbacks, the community will create a marvelous future based on nothing more than a dream. However, if you remove grace and replace it with a culture of guilt and blame, the experience of failure can paralyze a community. The feelings associated with failure, in a shame-and-blame context, become the fuel for self-abasement or self-justification. Either way, the community will find itself frozen in the past, unwilling or afraid to pick up the pieces and try again. I know this from personal experience! When our community found itself in such a spot it was nearly impossible for us to find the emotional energy or the will to press on and start over.

I have a tendency to waste time ruminating on the past. It's not the best character trait for someone who secretly dreams of being a futurist. I love being around those kinds of people—innovators who have one hand on the pulse of social trends, an eye on shifts in the culture, and the leadership capacity to inspire others to create a future based on informed vision and shared values. On my best days I operate in the present with an eye on the future. But during this season—when the community I loved was unraveling—I got stuck in the past, rehearsing regrets and replaying scenarios in my mind of what I should have said or done differently. I was stuck in grief.

I know this to be true about myself: when I dwell on mistakes I've made in the past, sadness hovers over my heart like a dark cloud. If I'm preoccupied with urgent demands in the present, anxiety railroads my emotions. However, when I dream about the future, my heart becomes energized and hopeful. I'm at my best when I live in the moment, dreaming about the future as I work on a new endeavor with my friends. On days like that, I dream with my eyes wide open, keenly aware if we seize the moment together, the work we accomplish in the present will create the future we're dreaming about.

During, and long after, the community meltdown, I was heartsick and sulked for months on end. I'll never forget the day when my son Nathan confronted my prolonged grief. I was on the roof of my house cleaning leaves from the gutters. Nathan bounced out of the house with a book in his hand and said, "Dad, I know what your problem is." (To be candid, I didn't know I had a "problem" my son felt he needed to solve.) He was reading a book by Anne Lamott and said, "It's right here in the book—you have colorectal theology!" There was a long pause and then he pointed to the book and said, "Your head is so far up your own ass you offer hope to no one!"[7] I remember thinking: it's a good thing I'm up here and you're down there, because if you were up here with me I would throw your colorectal off the roof!

Sometimes the truth hurts. But most of the time truth is exactly what we need to hear. When it comes from the right person, spoken in the right way, with the right motives, truth can set you free. I had been self-absorbed for far too long. My spirit was downcast and hopeless. I was tired and stressed. I lost my vision and my hope for the future. Nathan was right. I needed to get my head out of my butt, look beyond myself, and see what God was doing—in, around, and through our community. It was time to forgive, release, and reengage life.

The folks who remained in the Promise community were ready and eager to refocus the vision and realign our values with the values of Jesus. It wasn't easy, nor did light return to the darkness overnight; however, as we began to savor the moment in the present, working side by side on our vision for the future—the vision of offering hope to a broken world, even though we ourselves were broken—healing and new layers of wisdom unfolded. Forgiveness and grace allowed us to learn from our mistakes and begin again with new insight.

Over time I began to realize that forgiveness and grace provides the opportunity for human beings—and communities—to live more integrated and authentic lives. A culture of grace creates the space where we no longer have to shun, nor be ashamed of, our failures. The shadow cast by our worst days can be integrated with the delightful beauty of our best. We are all a strange mix of saint and sinner. Because that is so, we must expect the same to be true for the communities we are a part of. We all experience seasons of joy and sadness, as well as seasons of success and failure. The communities we live in and the organizations we belong to will experience the same ebb and flow. Health and wholeness will forever elude us if are unwilling to integrate our shadow side with the divine light God has placed in our souls. When we learn to embrace our biggest failure alongside our greatest success, we are on the way to living a more holistic life.[8] Perhaps that's one

7. Lamott, *Bird by Bird*, 102.
8. Palmer, *On the Brink*, 173–76.

reason Jesus values forgiveness and new beginnings so deeply, and encourages us to do the same.

Colorectal Church

The life of the church and its role in the world are important to me; that's the main reason I constantly check for vital signs and critique the status of the church. Sometimes I look through a microscope and focus on one small missional community called Church of the Promise. When I do, I ask myself questions like the ones raised in this book. How is it with the soul of our local church? Are we aligning our values with the values of Jesus? Is our vision and mission in line with his? There are other times when I get out the telescope and observe the bigger picture, reflecting on the life of the universal church. When I do, my telescope usually focuses on the constellation of churches classified as evangelical. As I stated in the introduction, this is the constellation where I was raised—the place in the global church I consider home.

When I take a macro-assessment of the evangelical church and juxtapose it with the political climate and the prevalent culture of North America, I hear Anne Lamott's question ringing in my ear: are we "seeing things in such a narrow and darkly narcissistic way that [we] present a colorectal theology, offering hope to no one?"[9] The question is fair and timely: In this season of church history, do we evangelical Christians have our head stuck in our ecclesiastical butt? Have we become so internally focused that we fail to relate, in any applicable way, to the hurting world around us? Does the church offer hope? Or, do we have what Reggie McNeal calls "missional amnesia?"[10] Have we fallen asleep at the wheel and forgotten our mission?

The evangelical church in North America, for all practical purposes, has lost its prophetic voice. When observed through a macro lens, it is apparent that we no longer communicate our gospel of hope in a way that is heard or received by the majority of people outside the church. In many ways, the failure of the evangelical church to stay on course with the mission of Jesus has been an innocent diversion, following what we thought was helpful and right. We developed programs to attract people to our gatherings and failed to notice we were becoming consumer-driven rather than mission-focused. We bought into seeker-sensitive models of doing

9. Lamott, *Bird by Bird*, 102.

10. McNeal, *Missional Renaissance*, 64–65.

102

church so people would come to the worship service and not be challenged or offended, with a hope they would return. We became more and more interested in what we were doing inside the church walls with our church friends and lost focus on what was going down outside the church building. We naively bought into homogenous models of church growth, believing the larger the church, the more reason to claim vitality and success. The homogenous gatherings made it easy to deny or neglect the challenges of diversity in our culture and the racial unrest in the world around us. It all seemed right because a significant number of people were responding to our message and what we offered to the community felt wholesome—at least to those who were coming to the church meetings.

Now is the time for a new beginning. The stakes are too high to merely play church. We can no longer go through the motions of worship, meeting with our homogenous friends every week, pretending all is well with the world, with the church, and with our souls. We cannot squint our eyes at the light in order to blur the truth so it makes pretty shapes and colors. We must look at the truth with our eyes wide open. We can no longer pretend that we have been an obedient church, that we have loved our neighbors well, and responded with compassion to the cries of the needy. We cannot continue to give lip service to the prayers of confession, and week after week, month after month, wander up to the communion rail, slug down some bread and juice, and forever put off the hard work of repentance and making amends. It is time for church leaders, clergy and lay alike, to realign the church with our apostolic mission.

There are multiple layers where the church has muddled the gospel of Jesus with our own need for social privilege and political power. Rather than being a prophetic voice that holds imperial forces to account, we aligned the church with partisan politics. We confused nationalism and patriotic commitments with allegiance to Jesus, allowing the former to trump the latter. We diluted the values of Jesus, making it easier to follow him while pursuing the American dream. We presented an ethos of separatism and paternalism, creating a brand the world views as judgmental. How can it be that a group of people who follow Jesus of Nazareth—the one who values extravagant grace, the champion of forgiveness and new beginnings—are dismissed from public discourse because of our judgmental spirit?

The strategy for regaining our prophetic voice and fulfilling our mission will not be found in attempts to make America—or the church for that matter—great again. We will not reclaim our apostolic heritage, nor live into our mission, if the goal is to push our way back into the center of community conversations, demanding political power and social position. On the contrary, it is from the margins of society, in a place of brokenness and humility, that we will find our way forward.[11] We must go backward if we want to go forward. We must go back and reclaim what was left behind.

The word *sankofa*, spoken by the Akan tribe in Ghana, can help point the church in the right direction. The word literally means "go back and get it," and is associated with the axiom: "It is not taboo to fetch what is at risk of being left behind." The Akan people created an image to represent the importance of *sankofa*. The symbol is a mythical bird, with its feet planted and facing forward while its head is turned backward retrieving an egg. The Akan believe the past is the best guide when planning the future.[12] If we fail to learn from history, we will repeat the mistakes we made in the past. But if we revisit the past, name and confess our failures, examine the choices we made and the motives we had for making them, and consider how to make amends in the present, the wisdom we gain will lead us into a stronger future.

The evangelical church would be wise to go back and fetch what is at risk of being left behind. I cannot speak for the church as a whole, but I can speak from my own perspective. When I take my head out of my own butt and look around, it seems obvious to me that the evangelical church has left behind the real values of Jesus. When I look at my evangelical church, I have to wonder if we take Jesus seriously. Do we really believe he meant the things he said? It seems to me that we have Americanized the gospel, making it more about personal self-fulfillment than the well-being of the community, favoring upward mobility at the expense of others. We have traded our prophetic voice for political position and privilege. We have neglected to love the poor. We have drawn lines in the sand separating us from *those people*—the ones with whom we disagree—and in so doing we've made enemies we fail to love. In the distant and recent past, when social injustice brought harm to our brothers and sisters, we were strangely silent, failing to advocate for the oppressed. In our enthusiasm to share the gospel of Jesus we have discounted the experience of others, causing harm and pushing people further away from the good news we wish to share.

You may or may not agree with my assessment of the church. But I do believe an honest evaluation of the evangelical church in North America

11. Hirsch, *Forgotten Ways*, 30.
12. Berea College, "Power of Sankofa," lines 1–19.

will reveal that we have failed to live and love like Jesus. If we want to regain our prophetic voice and live into our apostolic mission, we would do well to confess our failures, learn from our mistakes, and reclaim the values of Jesus. If we do, a stronger and more prolific future awaits us. We can rest assured—with confidence and hope—when we humble ourselves before the Lord and one another, God will meet our failures with extravagant grace and lead us into a new beginning.

A New Beginning

When I think about new beginnings, I usually think about individuals making a fresh start; but here lately, I've been asking myself: what does it look like for an organization to make a new beginning? How does a corporate group of people learn from its mistakes, make amends to the people they've harmed, and begin again with a more healthy approach to their stated purpose?

I wrote a simile to help answer the question: *Character is to an individual as culture is to an organization.* If a shift in the core identity of an individual (values, beliefs, and behaviors) leads to the transformation of personal character, it stands to reason that a shift in the core identity of an organization (group norms of behavior and the underlying values that keep those norms in place) will lead to a transformation of the organization's culture.[13] Transformation is possible for individuals. It is possible for organizations. And it is possible for the church.

The leadership of an organization can initiate a transformation in culture. However, corporate change will also happen—perhaps more effectively—if a significant number of people from within the organization adopt a new value system and then begin to think, talk, and behave in ways that reinforce the new preferred values. Therefore, if a collective mass of people from within the church will simply go back and reclaim the values of Jesus, and then align the way they think and the way they tell the Christian story with the words and ways of Jesus, the culture of the church will shift. If the new values and the new narrative are reinforced with new behaviors and the new behaviors produce the desired outcomes, the potential to influence and sustain a new culture in the larger organization will increase greatly.[14]

13. Kotter, "Key to Changing," lines 14–15.
14. Kotter, "Key to Changing," lines 29–36.

Creating culture sounds exciting and adventurous. The idea of a Spirit-led movement that reshapes the culture of the church makes the hairs on the back of my neck stand on edge with electricity. Even as I write these words, my heart races a bit and my mind begins to imagine what our city will be like when the church begins to look like Jesus! It makes me want to get up and do something . . . and then reality interrupts the adrenaline rush. Changing culture is by no means an easy endeavor, especially when you're talking about changing the culture of the church. Old paradigms have staying power, even when you want to change. Add sacred tradition, faith talk, and religious experience to the culture you want to change, and it becomes nearly impossible to shift from an old narrative to a new and more vibrant one.

There is yet another dynamic that frustrates paradigm shifts within the church, or any organization for that matter. Organizational leaders deceive themselves when they think they can manage their way into a desired future. The culture of an organization will never change as the result of a fine-tuned strategic plan, even when the plan includes fancy graphs and a list of corporate values. I have sat in countless meetings with other church leaders, discussing the nature and current condition of the church. We talk about the need for change. We point out what's wrong. We even spend time listing out on flip charts our hopes and dreams for the future. After the meeting, we return home, roll up our sleeves, and get busy . . . managing this week's problems and programs. Robert Quinn, author of *Deep Change*, says, "It is much easier to focus on solving today's problems than it is to mold the future. It is easier to be an operational analyzer and taskmaster than it is to be a developmental and visionary motivator."[15]

Deep change in an organization takes place when people have the guts and the tenacity to align their behaviors with a new set of preferred values. Organizational change will not shift by simply writing down a list of corporate values and expecting others to adopt them. People who desire the change must identify the gap between the "real values" of the organization and the "preferred values" and then be resilient enough to modify their behavior to reduce the gap between the two. The church is in desperate need of adaptive leaders and visionary motivators who will create microcosmic models of what the church can look like if we change the narrative and align our behavior with the values of Jesus.

15. Quinn, *Deep Change*, 198.

Shane Claiborne, founder of The Simple Way, describes a time, in his book *The Irresistible Revolution,* when he and his friends decided to stop complaining about the church they saw and set their hearts on becoming the church they dreamed of.[16] The book is a beautiful story of what the church can look like when a small group of people value the things Jesus values and then set out to find ways to align their storytelling and their behaviors with the new—or should I say old—*red-letter values of Jesus.*

People don't agree on much these days, but I think most would affirm that the world is in a mess. People are hungry for a taste of hope. We are desperate for a glimpse of what Jesus envisioned when he talked about the kingdom of God. Both the church and the world need to see expressions of genuine Christian community. Perhaps you and a handful of friends can reimagine what the church could look like in your context? The change you dream about will begin to emerge as you organize your common life around the values of Jesus. Below are seven questions to help set the dream in motion:

- What would it look like if you and your friends decided to love God with all your heart, soul, mind, and strength, and to really love your neighbor as you love yourself?

- What would be different if you decided to make your love for people who live on the margins of your community the matrix to measure how well you love God?

- What would change if you and your friends decided to follow the descending way of Jesus?

- If you decided to affirm the dignity of all people the way Jesus did, what would change in your disposition towards people who are different from your affinity group?

- How would you use your resources differently if you decided to adopt the radical generosity of Jesus?

- What small step can you and your friends make today to let the world see a church that looks like Jesus?

- What hurt, resentment, or failure stands in the way of you chasing after the new beginning God wants to bring about in your life?

16. Claiborne, *Irresistible Revolution,* 64.

Jesus is inviting you to follow him. If you take him up on the invitation and begin to take his words and his ways seriously, you will learn how to live and love like him. You and your friends can reimagine a church that looks like Jesus, creating a culture where the vision of Jesus is seen and felt by the people in your neighborhood. Come on, let's follow Jesus together on a mission to love God and love our neighbors, every day!

RED LETTER QUESTIONS

Woman, where are they? Has no one condemned you?

1. In John 8:1–11, we are placed in the middle of a story where two distinct cultures collide. On the one hand, we encounter a culture of shame and blame, represented by the religious leaders. On the other, we experience a culture of grace and new beginnings, expressed in the way Jesus responds to the religious leaders and the woman caught in adultery. Take a moment to compare and contrast the two cultures.

2. When Jesus stoops down to doodle in the dirt, he responds to the drama with a non-anxious presence. His action deescalates the tension and creates a protected space for the woman. Before you and your group evaluate your successes and failures, your group norms, and the values you hold to keep those norms in place, what can you do to create a protected space? Here are a few suggestions: agree to refrain from casting blame on past failures. Agree to resist self-justification and making excuses for past mistakes. Make a covenant to affirm the dignity of all group members.

3. Take some time to evaluate and reflect on your core identity. Do the same for your group.

   • What are your values and beliefs, and how are they reflected in your behavior?

   • What are the norms of your group and what values does your group embrace to keep those norms in place?

   • Where have you or your group failed to align with the values of Jesus?

   • Where have you or your group reflected the values of Jesus?

   • Name a few of your successes.

   • Name specific programs, projects, or social positions you or your group has taken that failed to represent the way of Jesus.

   • Try to imagine new ways of organizing your group around the values of Jesus.

4. In light of your evaluation, are there things you should *stop* doing?

5. Is there something new you should *start* doing?

7

Red Letter Vision: A Healing Land

"If I paint a wild horse, you might not see the horse, but surely you will see the wildness!"

PABLO PICASSO

"If you want to build a ship, don't drum up [men and women] to gather wood, divide the work and give orders. Instead, teach them to yearn for the vast and endless sea."

ANTOINE DE SAINT-EXUPERY

"The time has come; the kingdom of God has come near. Repent and believe the good news!"

JESUS

VISION IS A PRECIOUS gift, an expression of love given to us from the heart of the most creative person in the universe. The ability to see the beauty of God's creation with our eyes and to savor the majestic shapes and colors of life in our minds is a breathtaking wonder, one that causes me to pause often and say, "Thank you!"

The beauty of life is indeed a grand display of God's creative love—and it blows my mind. When I consider all of the things God created, what really makes my head spin is the fact that God created you and me in God's image, with the ability to create. God has fashioned humans in such a way that we have the potential to see things that are invisible; to have a vision of something that is not yet and work with our hands to bring the invisible vision into visible reality.

Sandcastles and Invisible Kingdoms

Every year when my children were young, we would spend an entire day of our summer vacation creating something out of nothing. Well, that's not quite true. God did supply the sand. But we accessed our gift of vision, along with plastic buckets and shovels, to create expressions of art for other families on the beach to enjoy. Creating sand sculptures with my children was a highlight of my summer vacations, one I'll savor in memory for years to come. As soon as Kathie and I set the date and zeroed in on the destination, the kids would begin dreaming about our next masterpiece.

Most folks limit themselves to sandcastles; turning buckets of sand upside down, adorning the bucket-shaped pile of sand with seashells and digging moats to protect the blob of sand from the rising tide. We did our share of simple sandcastles, but our specialty was the animal kingdom, specifically creatures from the sea world. We created larger-than-life sea turtles, king snow crabs, dolphins leaping out of the sand, and a walrus with ivory tusks, sipping on a Bud Light.

The largest of all was the fifteen-foot lobster, with pincers the size of a Volkswagen, positioned and ready to bite any child who dared to walk across the lobster's back. The most elaborate creation was the mermaid, lying under an umbrella with a bottle of suntan lotion by her side and a glass of lemonade in her hand. She had seaweed dreadlocks for hair and turquoise-colored seashells for eyes. I'm pretty certain the mermaid was the most photographed attraction on the beach the entire summer.

At the beginning of our sand-sculpting career, Nathan was too small to wield his plastic shovel as a sculptor wields a chisel, so he was commissioned to dig holes, fetch water, and look for much-needed accessories like shells and seaweed. Nathan would putter around in the sand and chase seagulls while Ryan and I tended to the intricate details. When I look back and consider all the castles and sculptures we made, they all fade in comparison to one brilliant expression of art created by Nathan at the age of five.

As we finished the final details on a starfish, Nathan grabbed my hand, and with eyes the size of two Frisbees, he announced: "Look, Dad! It's an amusement park!" All I saw was a mound of sand as high as Nathan's knees, spreading out three feet in diameter. He then proceeded to walk me through the amusement park. "You buy your ticket here before you go in. The roller coaster is over here and there's the merry-go-round. You play games and win stuffed animals over here. There's the petting zoo and there's the cotton candy machine and a place to eat snow cones. Before you go out the back door you get to walk through the gift shop and buy a souvenir."

It was all there, two inches under the sand, visible for everyone to see—all you needed was the imagination of a five-year-old. Nathan and Walt Disney had a lot in common—the ability to see invisible kingdoms. Walt Disney, like Nathan, looked at a swamp in central Florida and saw a magical kingdom, a place where the whole world would vacation and give him their life savings.

A Love for the Sea

Whenever I think about Nathan's amusement park, I'm reminded of Antoine de Saint-Exupery's book *The Little Prince*. It is absolutely my favorite children's story of all time. It was on the required reading list for all three of my children and will be read more than once to each of my grandchildren.

Like Nathan and Walt Disney, the Little Prince was able to see invisible things—things adults once saw when they were young but lost the capacity to see when they grew up. The Little Prince was able to look at a picture of a box with three holes drawn on the side, and see a sheep inside of the box taking a nap. When the Little Prince looked at a picture of what appeared to be a hat to all the grown-ups, he saw a boa constrictor digesting an elephant. When grown-ups, according to the Little Prince, became preoccupied with "matters of consequence," they forgot how to marvel at the wonders of life. They forgot how to press their noses against the windowpanes of life.[1]

Somewhere along the way, grown-ups lose the ability to perceive the invisible kingdom swirling around them, a kingdom filled with beauty and truth. Invisible things like the kingdom of heaven and eternal things like

1. Saint-Exupery, *Little Prince*, 7–8, 12, 71–73.

faith, hope, and love are perceived more with the heart than with the eyes. Perhaps this is why Jesus said, "Unless you change and become like little children, you will never enter the kingdom of heaven."[2]

How then, do we adults, who are consumed with matters of consequence—placing all of our attention on the temporal things of this world—learn to see eternal and invisible kingdoms? It's the same question Nicodemus asked Jesus on the night when they talked about eternal life. After Jesus said, "No one can *see* the kingdom of God unless they are born again," Nicodemus was perplexed and asked, "How do we, once we are grown become born again?" The answer to the riddle lies in what we long for—what we value over and above all other things. Jesus told Nicodemus, "Flesh gives birth to flesh, but Spirit gives birth to spirit."[3] If you want to see the invisible kingdom of heaven, you must be born of the Spirit; you must hunger and thirst for the eternal things that Jesus valued and long to see the things he saw.

Jesus said those who hunger and thirst for righteousness will be satisfied;[4] and he taught his friends if they seek first the kingdom of heaven, everything they need to live abundant and meaningful lives in this temporal world would be provided.[5] Long for heaven, have an appetite for righteousness and justice, and you will not only value the things Jesus valued, you will begin to see the invisible kingdom of heaven unfolding right before your eyes. More than that, the beauty of the kingdom will be set loose inside of you. Seeing the kingdom of heaven really is a matter of values and vision. It matters what or whom you place at the center of your life; and it makes all the difference whether you set your vision on temporal or eternal things.

Passions of the heart and the dreams we cherish will determine the lives we live and how we see the world. Jesus is letting Nicodemus and the rest of us in on a little secret: what we value will govern the way we live, the content of our dreams, and how we view the world. Our values and our vision for the future can place limits around our experience, or they can open us up to the invisible kingdom of heaven. On the one hand, if we are only concerned with matters of the flesh, we will focus our lives on the temporal. We will only see and be driven by what the Little Prince called "matters of consequence." On the other hand, if we are born of the Spirit and allow

2. Matt 18:23.
3. John 3:1–21.
4. Matt 5:6.
5. Matt 5:33.

our dreams and our deepest longings to be inspired by the Spirit of Christ, we will see an impending glimpse of heaven everywhere we walk and that vision will shape the world in which we live.

A beloved community that yearns to live and love like Jesus will fix its eyes on heavenly things and will learn to see the world through his eyes. The hopes and dreams of Christ will captivate our hearts, causing us to customize our community in a way that best reflects his vision for the world. We will chase after his vision with every ounce of energy we have.

One of the things that makes Jesus the world's greatest leader—beside the fact that he died and came back to life, canceling the power of sin and death—is his ability to cast a compelling vision. His vision for the world has captured the imagination of every generation since he walked on the planet. The difference between most religious leaders I know and the visionary leadership of Jesus is found in a quote by the author of *The Little Prince*: "If you want to build a ship, don't drum up [men and women] to gather wood, divide the work and give orders. Instead, teach them to yearn for the vast and endless sea."[6] The former leader is a taskmaster, the latter a visionary motivator. One builds ships; the other leads people into the great unknown of the deep and mysterious sea.

Jesus was far from being your run-of-the-mill religious taskmaster. He was a prophetic visionary to say the least! But he was more! He was a servant-leader who painted a compelling vision of a new future and then led the way, through self-giving sacrifice, to make his vision a reality. When he spoke, people were astonished at his words; they marveled at his wisdom and many abandoned their way of life to follow his. Jesus spoke in parables, told stories, and painted word pictures of what heaven was like. He described a place where good news would be preached to the poor, the blind would see, the oppressed and the prisoner would be set free. Righteousness, justice, and peace would flourish. He saw a time when joy would be the norm and everyone on the face of the planet would be invited to a festive celebration of Jubilee. Best of all, he insinuated that with his presence, the time had come for this *kingdom-of-heaven-on-earth* to begin. Those who followed him were invited to help make these realities of heaven an ever-present reality on earth.

What a wild and mysterious vision! The kingdom of heaven let loose on earth, permeating every crack and crevice in the world![7] How could we

6. Book Browse, "Book Browse Favorite Quotes," lines 1–2.

7. McNeal, *Missional Communities*, 37.

ever settle for building institutions and consumer-driven churches when the kingdom of heaven on earth is what Jesus had in mind? Do you want to build ships? Or do you want to follow Jesus into the vast and endless sea?

The Promise of a Healed Land

On the first Sunday of 2001, three of us decided to take Jesus up on his invitation. We didn't want to start a new program or create anything that resembled the typical "church-shaped" boat. We simply wanted to follow Jesus into the mysterious sea he was urging us to explore. We didn't set out to plant a church, but we felt compelled to meet on Sunday mornings and pray together. The plan was to meet, play a few worship songs on the CD player, read Scripture corporately, and listen to hear what God might say. Tony, a youth worker at the Promise Center; Jimmy, one of the teenagers from the neighborhood; and I decided to meet every Sunday for a year and follow this simple plan: meet, read, pray, listen. At the first meeting Tony said, "So what if nothing happens? If we meet every week for a whole year and pray, by the end of year we will have had a nice prayer meeting."

The three of us met faithfully for six weeks. On week seven we doubled in size—Kathie and my two sons decided to join us. Every Sunday we followed the same rhythm. We met, we listened to a few songs, we read Scripture, we prayed, and then we asked one another a simple question: How has God been getting your attention this week? By the time summer rolled around, there were a dozen neighbors meeting with us for prayer, with a few curious folks stopping in now and then to see what we were up to. There was no fanfare, no plan of action, just a handful of folks meeting for prayer and trying to hear God's voice.

In the middle of the summer a theme began to unfold. It felt as if God was pointing out a specific Scripture for us to grapple with. Over the course of seven weeks, a new person would wander into the meeting and say something like, "This week I've been reading 2 Chronicles 7:14," or, "As we were praying, 2 Chronicles 7:14 kept coming to my mind." By week five the group would laugh out loud as the new person to the conversation began to read, "If my people, who are called by my name, will humble themselves and pray and seek my face and turn from their sin, then I will hear from heaven, and I will forgive their sin and will heal their land."

The experience was so profound; we received the verse as a direct promise from God. Second Chronicles 7:14 was for us and for our neighborhood! The vision and the promise of a "healed land" began to work its way into every conversation we had. The verse became a foundational Scripture that grounded our life and work for the next fifteen years. We even changed the name of our non-profit community center from the Portland United Methodist Center to the Portland Promise Center to remind ourselves of the vision and the promise. By the end of the year we knew beyond a shadow of a doubt that we were called by God's name to be a kingdom-centric church that would co-labor with God and with one another to pursue a specific vision and a promise—a vision that said, *Portland will be a healed land; a place where families flourish and the peace of God is present.*

We plastered the vision everywhere: on the walls, on the website, on the doorpost, on our children's foreheads. The vision of a healed land resonated in our bones. It felt right and rang true. In a neighborhood like ours, where the weight of economic and health disparity looms like a dark cloud, the thought of a healed land brought renewed energy and focus to our work. However, for a vision to be helpful you need benchmarks along the way to know if you're moving in the right direction, towards the vision. "A healed land where families flourish and the peace of God is present" is fun to read when it's stamped on your child's forehead, but what does it really look like? How do you know when you've arrived at such a place? As we pressed ourselves to answer the question, we found Isaiah's vision of a new earth to be extremely helpful:

> 17See, I will create new heavens and a new earth. The former things will not be remembered, nor will they come to mind. 18But be glad and rejoice forever in what I will create, for I will create Jerusalem to be a delight and its people a joy. 19I will rejoice over Jerusalem and take delight in my people; the sound of weeping and of crying will be heard in it no more. 20Never again will there be in it an infant who lives but a few days, or an old man who does not live out his years; the one who dies at a hundred will be thought a mere child; the one who fails to reach a hundred will be considered accursed. 21They will build houses and dwell in them; they will plant vineyards and eat their fruit. 22No longer will they build houses and others live in them, or plant and others eat. For as the days of a tree, so will be the days of my people; my chosen ones will long enjoy the work of their hands. 23They will not labor in vain, nor will they bear children doomed to misfortune; for they will be a people blessed by the Lord, they and their descendants with them. 24Before they call I will answer; while they are still speaking I will

hear. 25The wolf and the lamb will feed together, and the lion will eat straw like the ox, and dust will be the serpent's food. They will neither harm nor destroy on all my holy mountain, says the Lord.[8]

Isaiah's is a holistic vision that covers every aspect of community life. A time is coming, says Isaiah, when all things will be new and set right. Joy and celebration will be the norm for community life (vv. 18–20). Both the young and the old will live long and healthy lives. Everyone will have access to affordable health care (v. 20). Decent and affordable housing options and employment opportunities will leave no one unhoused or forced to live in substandard housing (v. 21). No one will go hungry or live under the heavy burden of food insecurity (v. 22). Everyone will be gainfully employed, earning a livable wage, able to supply for their own needs (vv. 21–22). Family and spiritual support systems will be strong and viable (v. 23). Hearts of peace will replace hearts at war. Domestic violence, criminal violence, mass shootings, capital punishment, and war will be a thing of the past—a distant memory (v. 25). It's all there in Isaiah's vision: God's new earth will be a *healed land where families flourish and the peace of God is present.*[9]

Isaiah's prophetic vision is an eschatological passage, pointing to a time when God will establish the kingdom of heaven in its fullness, but Ray Bakke's commentary on this passage makes it difficult for anyone to simply dismiss Isaiah's vision as a utopian dream of the afterlife. In his book, *A Theology as Big as the City*, Bakke says, "If this is what God says a city ought to look like, and if God's Spirit lives in me, this is what I want [my city] to look like. For me, it's not enough to measure growing churches in the city. This text forces me to look also at the social side effects of churches filled with urban disciples of Jesus."[10]

Once we embraced Isaiah's description of God's new earth as our picture of what Portland would and should look like, the implications were huge. Any movement towards meeting one of these social or spiritual needs would be a step in the right direction; but addressing only one of these concerns would not create a healed land. For a beloved community to embrace this scale of mission, the approach had to be holistic. Our strategy needed to include a host of relational networks with other agencies, community developers, local churches, and individuals to work in concert for the well-being of the neighborhood. Portland didn't need another church; it

8. Isa 65:17–25.

9. Bakke, *Theology as Big as the City*, 81–83.

10. Bakke, *Theology as Big as the City*, 83.

needed a kingdom-centric movement, initiated by God and God's people—a movement that would address the social and spiritual issues of injustice, as well as personal and corporate sin that oppressed our neighbors and diminished their lives.[11]

Jesus got our attention by presenting us with an invitation to pray and seek God's face. He then challenged us to pursue a wild and mysterious vision of a healed land. Twenty years later, there's still a humble group of folks meeting on Sunday morning to sing a few songs, read Scripture, pray, and listen for God's voice. We still believe in the promise of God's new heaven and a new earth. Isaiah's vision is still in our sights for what Portland will look like someday. But we talk a little differently about our vision these days. Instead of referring to our neighborhood as a healed land, we now see a day when Portland will be known as a *healing land*.

From a Healed Land to a Healing Land

"Follow the people with the smiles and you'll wind up in Portland." That's what we want to hear people say about our neighborhood and Church of the Promise. Rather than a place to be avoided or a place in need of healing, we believe a time is coming when our neighborhood will be the desired place to live in our city. Because of our social and economic diversity, the historical DNA we bring to our city, and the unique blend of characters that live here, Portland is an amazing place to call home. For a while now, I've been predicting that Christians from churches on the suburban side of our city will come to the west side to do "mission work" only to find, and be surprised by, a healthy and vital church—a church that looks more like the New Testament church in Jerusalem or Antioch[12] than the safe, sterile, homogenous churches that characterize our American suburbs.

Some of my neighbors have predicted a "spiritual revival" is coming to Louisville. (This is one thing I absolutely love about my charismatic friends: they are always waiting for the next big revival and pray like it's just around the corner.) My friend Dave says this revival will begin in our west end neighborhoods and move east. Hmm! How interesting would that be, if the churches on the "poor" end of Louisville led the city into a more healthy and holistic way of living and loving?

11. McNeal, *Kingdom Come*, 4–10.

12. Acts 2:42–47; 4:32–37; 11:19–30.

When the social systems that support a community are broken, they should be fixed. If a community is unhealthy, measures should be taken to restore its health. But in the meantime, broken and unhealthy social systems do not determine the community's ability to do miraculous work. A beloved community that lives and loves like Jesus in an under-resourced, low-income neighborhood can restore health and hope to individuals, they can work together to heal unhealthy social systems, and they can be a beacon of light and love for an entire city. There is a grand distinction between a vision of being a healed land and one that seeks to be a healing land. Let me explain how we stumbled onto the difference.

For eleven years the prayer movement that began in 2001 continued to meet in the gym of our non-profit community center. In addition to gathering for worship and prayer on Sunday mornings, this small group of folks led the Celebrate Recovery program on Thursday evenings, provided a volunteer force for the Center's after-school program, and dreamed up schemes to celebrate life in the neighborhood through community block parties and family events.

Kathie and her friend Jackie led a women's Bible study every Tuesday night for years. The women's Bible study was a highlight of my week. Ladies from the neighborhood would walk to our house, toting their Bibles and homemade refreshments. Nathan and I would sneak out the back door and go to the movie theater or head to our favorite place to play chess. The mall had a chessboard in the center of the food court with four-foot tall chess pieces. It was a blast to share a smoothie with my son, chat about middle-school life, and play chess with a knight's horse you could actually ride on. After the movie, or after Nathan beat me at chess, we would return home and munch on leftover snacks.

This eleven-year stretch was a great season of sharing life and love with our neighbors. Woven throughout our meetings and times of prayer was the vision of a healed land and the notion of creating a holistic strategy to reach the vision. We set our eyes on an abandoned warehouse down the street, believing it would be an ideal location for an economic development hub in the neighborhood. In the center of the warehouse would be a space set apart for worship and prayer. The combination of business and worship would help provide a spiritual foundation for other enterprises that came to the neighborhood in the future.

We bought the building and then wandered around like Moses in the wilderness for the next seven years, trying to figure out how to enter the "promised land." In 2012, the river finally parted and the community of faith moved into the building. For the first time in eleven years we began to wonder what it would look like if we became an "official" local church in our United Methodist denomination. Until then, we had been flying under the radar of the institution, calling ourselves a "community of faith." Now, we were chatting with conference leaders about planting a church. The prayer movement would no longer be a program of the Portland Promise Center meeting in the corner of our non-profit organization. We would be a local United Methodist Church, eager to play its part in building a network of community developers who would love our neighbors by loving our neighborhood together.

Twelve people were asked to serve on our church plant "design team." Tattoo Johnny was one of those leaders. My district superintendent was another. Becki was a friend of the Center and believed in our vision. Beyond being my boss, she was a personal friend with phenomenal leadership skills. I was proud when she agreed to help co-lead our planning process.

The first few meetings were dedicated to forming our team. We took turns sharing stories about how we came to be a part of the Promise Community design team. Tattoo Johnny told about the time he asked me what kind of church we were. He went into great detail, as he always did when telling stories. He said, "I asked Larry what kind of church we were and he said it doesn't really matter; but if somebody important asks, we're United Methodist." As he told the story, I was kicking him under the table and pointing to Becki. He finally looked under the table to see who was kicking him, then he looked at me pointing down the table, then he looked at Becki. Uncontrollable laughter filled the room as the light bulb came on over Tattoo Johnny's head. "Oh! She's the somebody important!"

The next order of business for the design team was to draft a written covenant, a mutual agreement to help raise the level of accountability for our work together. All of our district committees made covenants. And they all sounded pretty much the same: Be prompt. Be prepared. Be positive. Participate and be kind. Most would say something about loving Christ and keeping confidence. But drafting a written covenant was far from normal for this group of folks. Our covenant was unique. We called it the "Glory Covenant." We agreed with all the normal things, like being prompt, prepared, and positive. But my charismatic friends on the team added a little flare to our written document. In good covenantal language they said, "When the Holy Spirit moves we will all shout gloooory and dance the jiggedy-jig!" No one on the team had a clue what a jiggedy-jig looked like, but all twelve of us signed the covenant.

Believe it or not, it was during a mind-numbing discussion on neighborhood demographics when we learned the dance. After two hours of flipping through countless pages of charts and graphs, someone in the group pointed out that the Portland neighborhood had 10,000 residents. Immediately, Second John began pounding his fist on the table and humming Matt Redman's song "Ten Thousand Reasons." In a heartbeat, with no cue from anyone, we were on our feet dancing the jiggedy-jig. It looked like a scene from *West Side Story*. In unison, as if we spent days choreographing the dance, we were singing the song and dancing in circles around the table. Our Portland neighbors offered 10,000 reasons for our souls to sing. I looked over at Becki and heard her say, "Who are you people?" Before we started singing the second verse, she was on her feet, honoring the covenant.

The level of creative energy would rise to new heights every time this group gathered to dream about a beloved community, built on the values of Jesus. We were curious and wide open, seeking fresh ways to be and do church. We asked ourselves: What would it look like to wed business and ministry? What would change in our city if we filled the warehouse with like-minded organizations that shared common values and visions for the neighborhood? How can we *be the church* Monday through Saturday? Flip charts and Post-It notes filled the room; each note pad was covered with our crazy ideas and wild dreams.

During one of those deep-dive brainstorming conversations, we asked ourselves a shoot-for-the-moon, no-holds-barred question: If the kingdom of God came in its fullness tomorrow, what would change in our city? As we wrestled with the question, saying all the right things, Tattoo Johnny raised his hand. When he got everyone's attention he said: "I've got a word to share. I think God wants Portland to be more than a healed land. I think God is saying, 'We're going to be a *healing land*.'" When he finished sharing his word the atmosphere in the room shifted. It was far more than a simple shift in syntax. It was a new vision, with a new and fresh perspective. It was certainly a more honoring way to view our neighborhood and a more profound vision of the role Portland would play, on a global scale, in the future.

We started filling up our flip charts with phrases of what it meant to be a healing land. Somebody said: "People will walk by our warehouse and feel better. They won't even know why." Another person said: "It will be like in the book of Acts when the shadow of the apostles crossed over people and they were healed. People will walk in the shadow of our building and feel the healing presence of God." Another said: "When people come into our space, they will feel the peace and presence of the Holy Spirit."

As our work continued, the images of a healing land kept pouring out and the focus of the vision moved beyond the building and the neighborhood: "People will come to Portland from other places, spend a few months with us and then go home a healed person, taking what they learned to another city." "Our community will be a place where people crawl in and dance out." Some of my Twelve-Step friends said: "It will be like step twelve in A.A. Having had a spiritual experience as result of spending time in Portland, we will take the message of God's healing grace to other cities and practice the principles we learned here in all of our affairs."

The image of a healing land brought our vision for the future into the present. The new vision was more than a future reality we were trudging towards; it was a current reality we could live into and practice in the here and now. The vision was a vision of hope! Even when current reality contradicted our vision for the future, we could operate as a healing land in the face of the contradiction. A healing land happens when the hope of the risen Christ is set loose in the heart of a community. That's what we were after. We wanted to be more than a healed land; we wanted to be a healing land—a beloved community grounded in hope, living out a promised future in the present.

Compelling Visions Lead People into Uncharted Territory

The Gospel stories talk about three basic strategies Jesus employed to fulfill his mission: he preached good news to the poor, he taught about the kingdom of God, and he healed the sick.[13] Preaching, teaching, and healing were the core strategies of Jesus. They were the ways and means he manifested the not-yet kingdom of heaven in the here-and-now. It seemed right for us to adopt those three strategies as our own. If we were going to be a healed land in the future, we needed to affirm the healing power of Christ in the present and learn to steward all our resources in cooperation with the Holy Spirit. The vision of Portland becoming a healing land challenged us on multiple levels.

First, the vision challenged our theology. We needed a theology of hope; one that was grounded in more than wishful thinking or silly

13. Matt 11:1–6.

optimism based in superstition. We needed the brand of optimism that Dietrich Bonhoeffer exemplified and wrote about while imprisoned in the Nazi prisons.[14] Bonhoeffer spoke about authentic optimism as a "will for the future" that "should never be despised even if it is proved wrong a hundred times."[15] This brand of optimism, says Bonhoeffer, "is health and vitality."[16] For our beloved community to operate as a healing land, we needed a will for the future that was grounded in God's promises and God's acts in history. The words of Jesus, his healing miracles, and his death and resurrection provided a rock-solid ground on which we could place our hope. The work of the Holy Spirit in and through the followers of Jesus in the book of Acts provided an example of what was possible. If we wanted to be a community that looked like Jesus, we couldn't pick and choose what we wanted to emulate and what we wanted to dismiss. Even if God's miraculous activity displayed in the life of Jesus and the apostles didn't match our own, we couldn't dumb down our theology to match our experience. We needed to make room for the power and the presence of the Holy Spirit to intervene in and through our lives.

Second, the vision of a healing land challenged us to stretch our spiritual muscle. It would be necessary to heed the admonition of Saint Paul and learn to "pray in the Spirit on all occasions, with all kinds of prayers and requests."[17] To be a healing land mandated we continue to place the practice of prayer at the center of our community life. However, we were challenged to broaden our thoughts about prayer and our practice of it. Richard Foster's book on prayer was a helpful resource. In *Prayer: Finding the Heart's True Home,* Foster covers the movements of prayer throughout church history and classifies them in three categories: inward-focused prayers that seek personal transformation; upward-focused prayers that lead us deeper into intimacy with God; and outward-focused prayers, such as intercession, healing, and what some call spiritual warfare or authoritative prayers.[18] Keeping prayer at the center of our beloved community and having the resilience to pray without ceasing, even in the face of unanswered prayer, stretched our spiritual muscle.

14. Bonhoeffer, *Letters and Papers from Prison*, 15.
15. Bonhoeffer, *Letters and Papers from Prison*, 15.
16. Bonhoeffer, *Letters and Papers from Prison*, 15.
17. Eph 6:18.
18. Foster, *Prayer*.

Finally, the vision challenged us to be more courageous. To become a healing land would demand that we leverage our political, social, and spiritual capital to heal the broken systems in our city. In the sixth chapter of his Letter to the Ephesians, Saint Paul reminds the church that our struggle is not against flesh and blood, but against rulers, authorities, powers of darkness, and spiritual forces of evil. After Saint Paul identifies the source of our struggle, he admonishes the church to put on the armor of God and stand firm against the powers and principalities of this world.[19] A prophetic role of the church is to speak truth to power and be an agent of healing for those whose lives have been demeaned by the systems of evil and personal sin. A community that wants to look like Jesus will confront the forces of evil, stand firm in the face of social injustice, and be willing, if necessary, to be the answer to its bold prayers. It was obvious to me: if our fun-loving community of faith wanted to become a healing land, we needed to download a big dose of courage from heaven.

Since the day Tattoo Johnny shared his "word from God," our beloved community has grown in all three of these areas. On some days we hit the proverbial ball out of the park. On those days our hope is high, we pray bold prayers, and we find the courage to do the next right thing. On other days, we strike out. On those days, discouragement pulls us towards despair and we pray self-centered prayers that lack authority or power. Our courage goes out the window, leaving us frozen by a spirit of timidity. But looking back over the years, one thing is for sure: we are pressing on toward the vision.

We have set our sights on an invisible kingdom, one not made with hands; an unshakable kingdom that is pressing into our current reality, giving us the hope and the authority we need to be a healing presence in our sin-sick world. Even though we see this invisible kingdom through a hazy window, we believe that someday the vision will be crystal clear. Until that day comes, we will do everything we can to align our values with the values of Jesus and set our compass toward his wild and mysterious vision, believing that if we follow him together, as close as we can, he will teach us how to live and how to love like he did. If we pull it off, our community will be known as a healing land.

19. Eph 6:10–20.

124

RED LETTER QUESTIONS

Do you see anything?

The question Jesus asked the blind man, after he applied spit to his eyes and laid hands on him, is a great question to ask ourselves: Do you see anything? The man responded to Jesus and said, "I see people; they look like trees walking around." Jesus then touched the man a second time. After this second touch his eyes were opened, his sight was restored, and he saw everything clearly (Mark 8:22-26).

For many of us it takes a second touch from the hands of Jesus (or a third, or a fourth) before we see the people around us as more than objects. When we see people as objects, either standing in the way of what we're trying to accomplish, or as a means to help us achieve what we want, we fail to see the invisible kingdom of God in our midst. We need for Jesus to touch our eyes, a second time if necessary, so we can see the eternal value of every person we meet and the beautiful potential God has placed in the communities where we live. Once we perceive the eternal value of people and places, we will begin to see and articulate a compelling vision worth living for. Here are four different ways to ask the question Jesus presented to the blind man.

1. If the kingdom of God were to come in its fullness tomorrow, *do you see anything* in your city that would change?

2. When you look at your neighborhood, *do you see anything* that breaks God's heart?

3. When you look at your neighborhood, *do you see anything* that breaks your heart?

4. *Do you see anything* you can do to heal the broken hearts?

8

Red Letter Mission:
Live and Love Like Jesus

*"Go and make disciples . . . teaching them to obey everything
I have commanded you."*

JESUS

"As I have loved you, so you must love one another."

JESUS

*"We are a community of ordinary people, following Jesus together on a
mission to love God and love our neighbors, everyday."*

CHURCH OF THE PROMISE

WHEN WE GET HONEST about the values of Jesus, *doing what it takes to align
ours with his,* and once we get clear about his kingdom-of-heaven-on-earth
vision, *walking with him towards the vision until he brings the kingdom in
its fullness,* the potential for creative expressions of living on mission with
Jesus go through the roof. The sky becomes the limit on what we might do
and how we might live on purpose with him. No longer will followers of
Jesus limit their mission to the practice of consumer-based religion, growing church membership, or doing church programs, with church people,
on church property. Jesus didn't invite people to go with him to a church

service, nor did he suggest the keys to the kingdom are found in doing a laundry list of religious activities. On the contrary, the great proposal of Jesus was far more adventurous—and a lot more dangerous.

The Great Proposal

Jesus was quite clear about his intentions for those who would take him up on his great proposal. "Whoever wants to be my disciple," says Jesus, "must deny themselves and take up their cross and follow me. For whoever wants to save their life will lose it, but whoever loses their life for me will find it."[1] Dietrich Bonhoeffer explained it this way: "When Christ calls [people], he bids [them] come and die."[2] Great pick-up line, Jesus! Come and die? What kind of invitation is that?!

No doubt, his invitation can be intimidating. However, when we put the great proposal of Jesus in the context of what he valued, what he taught, how he lived, and how he died, we begin to realize his proposal is an invitation to exchange our meaningless, self-suffocating narcissism for an eternal and abundant life worth living. He is inviting us to learn how to live and how to love in a new way—a way that actually honors our Creator and blesses the lives of other people. Jesus is inviting all who would come to follow him on a mission to love God and love their neighbors, everyday. It is a mission worth living for! It is a mission worth dying for!

The course of study to prepare ourselves for the mission will teach us how to live and love like Jesus. The course is far more extensive than a six-week Bible study or a four-year seminary degree. There are no CliffsNotes on the subject. It's not a three-step, nine-step, or twelve-step program. To learn how to live on mission with Jesus is a lifelong process. The great proposal, which Jesus extends to every person on the planet, is to follow him on a journey—to go where he's going and to learn directly from him as we travel.

When Jesus says "Come follow me," I hear two things. First, I assume he is going somewhere and inviting me to come along. If I follow, eventually we'll wind up at the destination where Jesus is leading. Second, he's inviting me to be his apprentice. As I follow him to the mysterious location, I can watch how he lives, observe how he loves, and listen to what he teaches. Over time, I will learn how to do what he does, how to love like he

1. Matt 6: 24–25.
2. Bonhoeffer, *Cost of Discipleship*, 99.

loves, and how to teach others what he is teaching me. This is the simple, yet profound goal of discipleship: find someone who knows how to do what you want to learn and then spend time with them.

Jesus, more than anyone else in the history of the world, knew how to live life in God's kingdom. And he made a way for others to do the same. Every day of your life is an opportunity to spend time with Jesus, following him deeper and deeper into the kingdom of heaven on earth.[3] What you experienced and learned yesterday can be accessed and used to meet the challenges of today. As each day passes, Jesus will show you how to share the joy and the freedom of God's kingdom with others.

What a fascinating mission! Jesus is inviting you and your community of faith to continue what he started. You can follow him into the kingdom of God, the place he envisioned and set in motion for us when he walked on the planet. As you follow him into that beautiful and mysterious space, you will learn how to live and love like him. You will observe what he valued and make every effort to upgrade your values to match his. Love and friendship will become the core values of your life. You will be challenged to question upward mobility and begin to follow Jesus on a downward trajectory toward humility and serving the poor. Like Jesus, you will find yourself disturbed by the social inequity in our world. You will learn how to affirm the dignity of every person you meet. Every resource you have— your treasures, your talents, and your time—will be seen as a gift from God to be used to bless the lives of other people, especially those who are oppressed by the systems of this world and pushed to the margins of society. The Spirit of Christ will inspire your dreams. As you follow Jesus, your creative imagination will extend beyond your experience. Instead of shrinking back, you will be encouraged by Jesus to live into your dreams, taking one small step at a time. You will live free from guilt and shame because Jesus will reveal to you the depth of God's mercy. He will give you the courage to make amends and seek forgiveness when you offend others; and, he will supply the abundant grace you need to forgive and release others when they harm you. Every day will be pregnant with opportunity to learn new things about the kingdom of God. Even your mistakes will become curriculum for learning more about yourself and God's glory. When your best-laid plans fall apart, your friendship with Jesus will empower you to begin again. Jesus will give you the courage to get back up and do the next right thing.

Can you see the potential for creative expressions of Christian community wrapped up in the mission Jesus passed on to us? Groups of ordinary

3. Willard, *Divine Conspiracy*, 282–83.

people, like you and me, and the communities we live in, are invited to live on mission with Jesus. As we spend time with him every day of the week, we will discover innovative ways to express the kingdom of God in the neighborhoods where we live.

If the grand proposal of Jesus sounds good to you, a new way of living and loving is on the horizon. Follow Jesus as closely as you can and great things will come to light. The hope and the healing power of Jesus and the creative beauty that characterized his life will become evident in your life as well. His whimsical way of making God's love known will become your way of living and loving.

If your faith community decides to embrace the great proposal of Jesus, you will no longer be bound by consumer-based religion, or stuck on a mission to increase church membership. The focus of your mission will stretch beyond Sunday meetings or church-based programs. The Red Letter Mission of Jesus will set your community free to live on mission with Jesus every day of the week—every moment of the day. As you follow Jesus together, you will discover new and relatable ways to express the wonder of God's kingdom in your neighborhood.

My hope is that you and your community will "Think Red" as you follow Jesus on this adventure called life. Go ahead; follow him as closely as you can! Take him seriously. Believe he really wants you to do the things he said. If you give it a whirl, he will teach you how to live and how to love. Jesus will inspire and empower you through the presence of the Holy Spirit to discover prophetic and pioneering ways to love God and love your neighbors, every day. If you wonder what your community will look like, here's a clue: over time, you and your friends will begin to look like Jesus.

We're Gonna Do Something

Whenever I think about following Jesus on an adventure to a mysterious destination, emulating him and learning from him along the way, I'm reminded of my grandson's first experience at the rodeo. Alex was only five years old at the time, but he began preparing for the rodeo when he was three. His uncle was the most courageous bull-riding cowboy he knew. Actually, he was the only cowboy he knew. Kathie and I still scratch our heads and wonder how our son, who grew up in an inner-city neighborhood, wound up riding rough stock in the rodeo. We knew strange things happen to your children when they go off to college, but riding bulls with names like Death Train, Widow Maker, and Satan was not on the radar.

Whenever Uncle Ryan came home for a visit, he and my daughter's son Alex would go bull riding. The show they put on for the family was a captivating drama. Alex played the cowboy's role and was definitely the star of the show. Ryan played the bull. The cowboy would square up on the bull's back, grab the bull's shirt collar with one hand, and raise his other hand high in the air. Once the heels of his boots were firmly gripped around the bull's ribs, the cowboy would yell out, "Lets go, boys! Let's go!" For the next eight seconds the bull would kick, buck, and spin Alex all over the living room. When the buzzer went off, Alex would fly through the air and land on the couch or under the coffee table. Someone in the house would check to make sure no bones were broken and then Alex would hop up, climb on the bull's back, and do it all over again.

After two years of riding a make-believe bull, in the safety of his grandmother's living room, the day finally came for Alex to go to a real live rodeo. I can still see it in my mind's eye, as if it happened yesterday. We were sitting in the bleachers, as close as we could to the fence that encircled the arena. Ryan and Alex were even closer to the action, sitting on the fence. Their cowboy hats tilted in the same direction. Their boots were covered in dust and cow manure. They both wore studded cowboy belts, boasting buckles the size of car hubcaps.

Alex cheered as the winner of the barrel race took a bow and tipped her hat to the audience, and then the announcer invited all the children to join him in the center of the ring for a mutton busting competition. In unison, the two cowboys jumped off the fence and headed for the middle of the arena. With one hand holding tight to Uncle Ryan's hand, Alex spun his head around to look back over his shoulder. A grin covered his entire face and his eyes sparkled like the diamond studs on his belt. He shouted in a loud voice for his grandmother to hear, "Mimi, we're gonna do something!"

My grandson had no clue where he was going or what he was getting ready to do. But he did know who was leading the way. Alex knew they were going to "do something" and he felt in his gut the "something" was going to be good, probably exciting, and maybe even dangerous. He wasn't sitting on the fence any longer, watching others have all the fun. He wasn't pretending in the living room. He was following his favorite uncle into the arena, heading towards the action.

They call it mutton busting for a reason. One by one, the boys and girls were placed on the back of a sheep and told to hold on. Once they had a good grip, the sheep were set loose to run as fast as they could across the arena. Seconds later, the children riding on the sheep's back would go flying through the air—busting their butts on the ground.

We watched from the bleachers as Ryan lifted Alex in the air to set him on the sheep. He dug his fingers deep into the sheep's wool and hung on as tightly as he could. With his legs and arms flying in every direction, Alex had the ride of his five-year-old lifetime. The sheep ran straight for the fence, made a sudden stop, turned on a dime, and started running in the other direction . . . without Alex. When Alex hit the dirt, applause filled the arena. He jumped to his feet, wiped the dust from his jeans and flung his little cowboy hat into the air! Just like Uncle Ryan!

It's Time to Do Something Different

Jesus is inviting you to follow him. Where he's leading and what you'll do along the way remains a mystery. But you can rest assured, if you place your hand in his and follow him as closely as you can, he will lead you on a grand adventure. The invitation may sound intimidating; don't let fear of the unknown keep you from following him into a new and more exciting future. We've played around in the safety of God's living room long enough. We've spent far too much time sitting on the fence. It's time for the people who follow Jesus to get out of the church building and step into the arena of life—the arena Jesus called the kingdom of heaven. It's time for us to reimagine how to be on mission with Jesus, every day of the week, every moment of the day.

If you want in on the Red Letter Mission of Jesus, gather up a handful of friends and grab hold of life as tightly as you can. Begin to imagine how Jesus would live and love if he were living in your community. Who would he comfort? Who would he challenge? How would he spend his time and where would he invest his resources? What would break his heart and what would he do to heal the brokenhearted?

If you wrestle with these questions long enough and allow yourself to imagine new and creative expressions of church, the Holy Spirit will use your community to bless your city. You will become a place of hope and a means of healing for your neighbors. Your community will remind people of how beautiful Jesus really is, because you will begin to look like him. The world is waiting for people like you to grab the hand of Jesus and say out loud for all of us to hear: "We're gonna do something!"

RED LETTER QUESTIONS

When the Son of Man comes, will he find faith on the earth?

In Luke 18:1–8, Jesus tells a parable about perseverance, exhorting his followers to persist in the work of justice and prayer. In this parable, Jesus uses the art of comparison and contrast to highlight the difference between the unjust systems of this world and God's justice. Jesus teaches that God, unlike the judge in the parable, desires to bring justice quickly to those who cry out day and night. Jesus ends the parable with a question: "When the Son of Man comes, will he find faith on the earth?"

The parable, and the question at the end of the story, underscores the value Jesus places on equitable treatment of people, and highlights an expectation Jesus has for his followers. Jesus expects those who follow him to place a high value on social justice, and to pray and live faithfully towards that end. He expects us to continue what he started, to actually do the things he did, and to love others the way he loved us. When social evil prevents people from experiencing the abundant life of God's kingdom, Jesus expects his followers to do something about it.

1. To help define your mission, take a moment and meditate on the values of Jesus. Review the ones discussed in this book. Name other values of Jesus not mentioned here. How prevalent are these values in your community?

2. Take some time and talk with Jesus about his kingdom-of-heaven-on-earth vision. Where is the kingdom of God being expressed in your neighborhood? Where and how is God's kingdom life being diminished or frustrated in the lives of your neighbors?

3. As you follow Jesus into the kingdom of God, how might you and your beloved community express the values of Jesus in fresh and whimsical ways?

Connect with Other Communities Who Are Thinking Red

We find life is better when we dream together. If you have been intrigued by the ideas shared in this book or inspired to reimagine how your community will express the words and ways of Jesus, please visit our community at thinkredtogether.com. We want to hear about your dreams, stories of how thinking red is making a difference in your neighborhood will be an inspiration to others.

If you want to chat with Larry you can contact him at thinkredtogether.com/contact. He would love to hear from you. Larry is also available to meet with your church to help you reimagine how your community can live out the red-letter mission of Jesus. If you would like Larry to visit with your team or speak at your event, don't hesitate to contact him at Think Red Together.

Bibliography

Baker, John. *Celebrate Recovery: Leader's Guide.* Grand Rapids: Zondervan, 2005.

Bakke, Ray. *A Theology as Big as the City.* Downers Grove, IL: InterVarsity, 1997.

Berea College. "The Power of Sankofa: Know History." https://www.berea.edu/cgwc/the-power-of-sankofa/.

Blanchard, Ken, and Michael O'Connor. *Managing by Values: How to Put Your Values into Action for Extraordinary Results.* San Francisco: Berrett-Koehler, 2003.

Bonhoeffer, Dietrich. *The Cost of Discipleship.* New York: Collier, 1963.

———. *Letters and Papers from Prison.* Edited by Eberhard Bethge. New York: Simon and Schuster, 1997.

Book Browse. "Book Browse Favorite Quotes." https://www.bookbrowse.com/quotes/detail/index.cfm/quote_number/401/if-you-want-to-build-a-ship-dont-drum-up-people-but-rather-teach-them-to-long-for-the-endless-immensity-of-the-sea.

Boyle, Gregory. *Tattoos on the Heart: The Power of Boundless Compassion.* New York: Free Press, 2010.

Breen, Mike. *Building a Discipling Culture: How to Release a Missional Movement by Discipling People Like Jesus Did.* Pawleys Island, SC: 3DM, 2011.

Brown, Brené. *Daring Greatly: How the Courage to be Vulnerable Transforms the Way We Live, Love, Parent, and Lead.* New York: Gotham, 2012.

Brueggemann, Walter. *Celebrating Abundance: Devotions for Advent.* Compiled by Richard Floyd. Louisville: John Knox, 2017.

———. "The Liturgy of Abundance, the Myth of Scarcity: Consumerism and Religious Life." https://therivardreport.com/wp-content/uploads/2016/09/the_liturgy_of_abundance.pdf.

Burlingham, Bo. *Small Giants: Companies that Choose to Be Great Instead of Big.* New York: Penguin, 2005.

Claiborne, Shane. *Irresistible Revolution: Living as an Ordinary Radical.* Grand Rapids: Zondervan, 2006.

Claiborne, Shane, et al. *Common Prayer: A Liturgy for Ordinary Radicals.* Grand Rapids: Zondervan, 2010.

Collins, Jim. *Good to Great: Why Some Companies Make the Leap and Others Don't.* New York: Harper Collins, 2001.

Edison, Thomas. "Thomas Edison Quotes." https://www.goalcast.com/2017/05/11/thomas-edison-quotes-motivate-never-quit/thomas-edison-quotes-i-have-not-failed-ive-just-found-10000-ways-that-wont-work/.

Eldredge, John. *Beautiful Outlaw: Experiencing the Playful, Disruptive, Extravagant Personality of Jesus.* New York: Faith Words, 2011.

"Eleven Facts about Global Poverty." https://www.dosomething.org/us/facts/11-facts-about-global-poverty.

Fessler, Pam. "U. S. Census Bureau Reports Poverty Rate Down, but Millions Still Poor." *NPR.org*, September 10, 2019. https://www.npr.org/2019/09/10/759512938/u-s-census-bureau-reports-poverty-rate-down-but-millions-still-poor.

Ford, Henry, and Samuel Crowther. *My Life and Work.* Garden City, NY: Green Book, 1922.

Foster, Richard. *Prayer: Finding the Heart's True Home.* New York: Harper Collins, 1992.

Glover, Erika. "Live Like Mother Teresa, Finding Your Own Calcutta." *Franciscan Spirit* (blog), March 13, 2018. https://blog.franciscanmedia.org/franciscan-spirit/live-like-mother-teresa-finding-your-own-calcutta.

Harnish, James A. *Simple Rules for Money: John Wesley on Earning, Saving and Giving.* Nashville: Abingdon, 2009.

Hill, Brennan R., et al. *Faith, Religion and Theology: A Contemporary Introduction.* Mystic, CT: Bayard, 1990.

Hirsch, Alan. *The Forgotten Ways: Reactivating the Missional Church.* Grand Rapids: Brazos, 2006.

Hirsch, Alan, and Michael Frost. *The Shaping of Things to Come: Innovation and Mission for the 21st-Century Church.* Peabody, MA: Hendrickson, 2003.

Kettering, Charles F. "Science Quotes by Charles F. Kettering." Today in Science History. https://todayinsci.com/K/Kettering_Charles/KetteringCharles-Quotations.htm.

King Center. "The King Philosophy." https://thekingcenter.org/#the-beloved-community.

Kittle, Nick. "Succeed Fast by Failing Faster." Government Innovators Network, a Forum for Innovation in the Public Sector, Harvard Kennedy School, Ash Center for Democratic Governance and Innovation. https://www.innovations.harvard.edu/blog/succeed-fast-failing-faster

Kotter, John. "The Key to Changing Organizational Culture." *Forbes,* September 27, 2012. https://www.forbes.com/sites/johnkotter/2012/09/27/the-key-to-changing-organizational-culture/#62a374d55094.

Lamott, Anne. *Bird by Bird: Some Instructions on Writing and Life.* New York: Pantheon, 1994.

McNeal, Reggie. *Kingdom Come: Why We Must Give Up Our Obsession with Fixing the Church—And What We Should Do Instead.* Carol Stream, IL: Tyndale, 2015.

———. *Missional Communities: The Rise of the Post-Congregational Church.* San Francisco: Jossey-Bass, 2011.

———. *Missional Renaissance: Changing the Scorecard for the Church.* San Francisco: Jossey-Bass, 2009.

———. *Practicing Greatness: Seven Disciplines of Extraordinary Spiritual Leaders.* San Francisco: Jossey-Bass, 2006.

National Alliance to End Homelessness. "State of Homelessness: 2020 Edition." https://endhomelessness.org/homelessness-in-america/homelessness-statistics/state-of-homelessness-2020/.

Niebuhr, Reinhold. *The Essential Reinhold Niebuhr: Selected Essays and Addresses.* Edited by Robert McAfee Brown. Binghamton, NY: Vail-Ballou, 1986.

Nouwen, Henri J. M. *Here and Now: Living in the Spirit.* New York: Crossroad, 1994.

Palmer, Parker J. *On the Brink of Everything: Grace, Gravity and Getting Old*. Oakland, CA: Berrett-Koehler, 2018.

Perkins, John M. *Beyond Charity: The Call to Christian Community Development*. Grand Rapids: Baker, 1993.

Peterson, Eugene H. *A Long Obedience in the Same Direction: Discipleship in an Instant Society*. Downers Grove, IL: InterVarsity, 2000.

———. *The Message: The Bible in Contemporary Language*. Colorado Springs, CO: NavPress, 2003.

Quinn, Robert E. *Deep Change: Discovering the Leader Within*. San Francisco: Jossey-Bass, 1996.

Saint-Exupery, Antoine De. *The Little Prince*. New York: Harcourt Brace Jovanovich,1971.

Schultz, Thom. "The Shocking Truth about Church Budgets." *HolySoup.com*, August 6, 2013. https://holysoup.com/the-shocking-truth-of-church-budgets/.

Sider, Ronald J. *Just Generosity: A New Vision for Overcoming Poverty in America*. Grand Rapids: Baker, 1999.

Twiss, Richard. "CCDA National Conference 2011: Richard Twiss." https://www.youtube.com/watch?v=fGw7AU6VDOs&t=973s.

———. *One Church, Many Tribes: Following Jesus the Way God Made You*. Ventura, CA: Regal, 2000.

Unicef for Every Child. "Levels and Trends in Child Mortality." https://data.unicef.org/resources/levels-and-trends-in-child-mortality/.

Warren, Michelle Ferrigno. *The Power of Proximity: Moving beyond Awareness to Action*. Downers Grove, IL: InterVarsity, 2017.

Wesley, John. *The Works of the Rev. John Wesley, volume 8*. 14 vols. New York: J&J Harper, D&S Neall, and W. S. Stockton, 1827.

White, Charles. "What Wesley Practiced and Preached about Money." *Mission Frontiers*, September 1, 1994. http://www.missionfrontiers.org/issue/article/what-wesley-practiced-and-preached-about-money.

Willard, Dallas. *The Divine Conspiracy: Rediscovering Our Hidden Life in God*. New York: Harper Collins, 1966.

Yaconelli, Michael. *Messy Spirituality*. Grand Rapids: Zondervan, 2002.

Made in the USA
Las Vegas, NV
01 November 2021